AF575920

Sailboats

PHOTOGRAPHS BY

MICHAEL KAHN

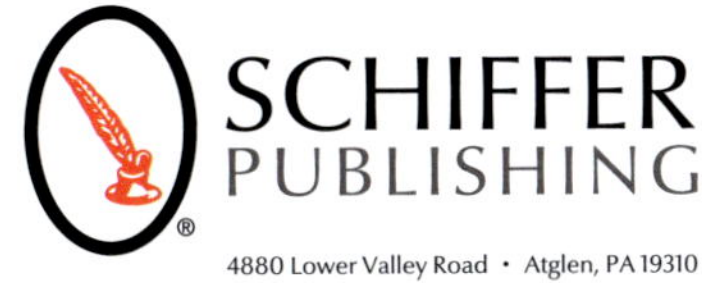

4880 Lower Valley Road • Atglen, PA 19310

INTRODUCTION

Combining my lifelong love of sailing and my passion for traditional black-and-white photography has led to this portfolio of classic sailing yachts. I believe these historic boats are some of the finest creations that man has ever made. Capturing these magnificent vessels in black-and-white film is the perfect marriage between history and technology.

While taking these photographs, there are many pieces that have to come together: wind, waves, clouds, lighting, and boat turnout. These elements blend together to create a handful of spectacular moments that can never be replicated on another day or another year. They are truly "one of a kind" moments in time.

Using antique camera equipment without motors or light meters means that I have just one chance to capture the moment before the boat goes by and I have to reposition myself on the next leg of the race. Knowing the course, the wind, and the lighting direction, I move around and wait for the boats to pass by me again. This cat-and-mouse chase goes on for several hours and can leave you exhausted. But while I am working on the water, it is quite exhilarating.

Through these photographs, I hope to invoke a sense of the thrill, beauty, history, and magic of these magnificent sailing vessels.

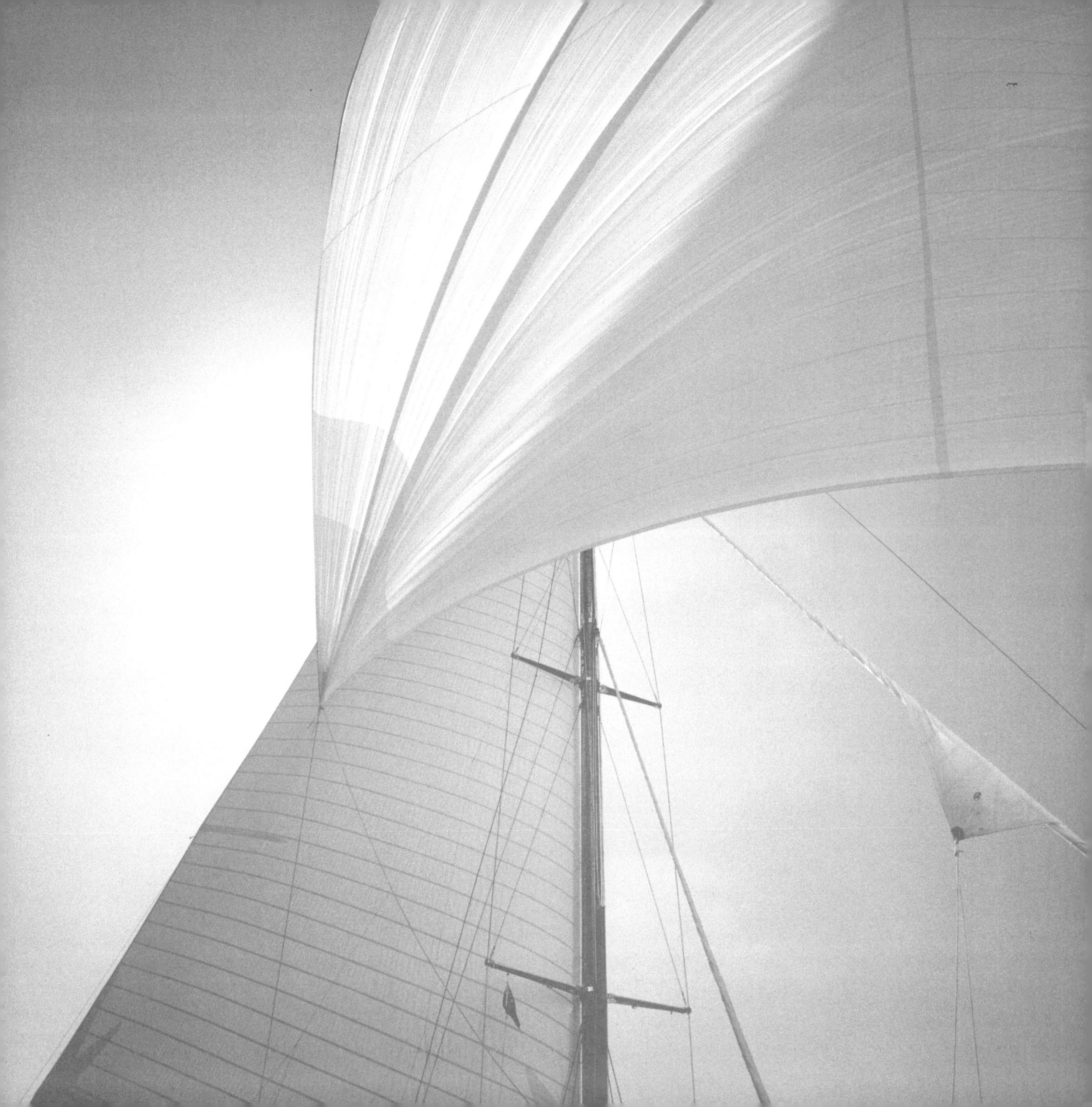

On a day
when the wind is perfect,
the sail just needs to open and
the world is full of beauty.
Today is such a day.

—RUMI

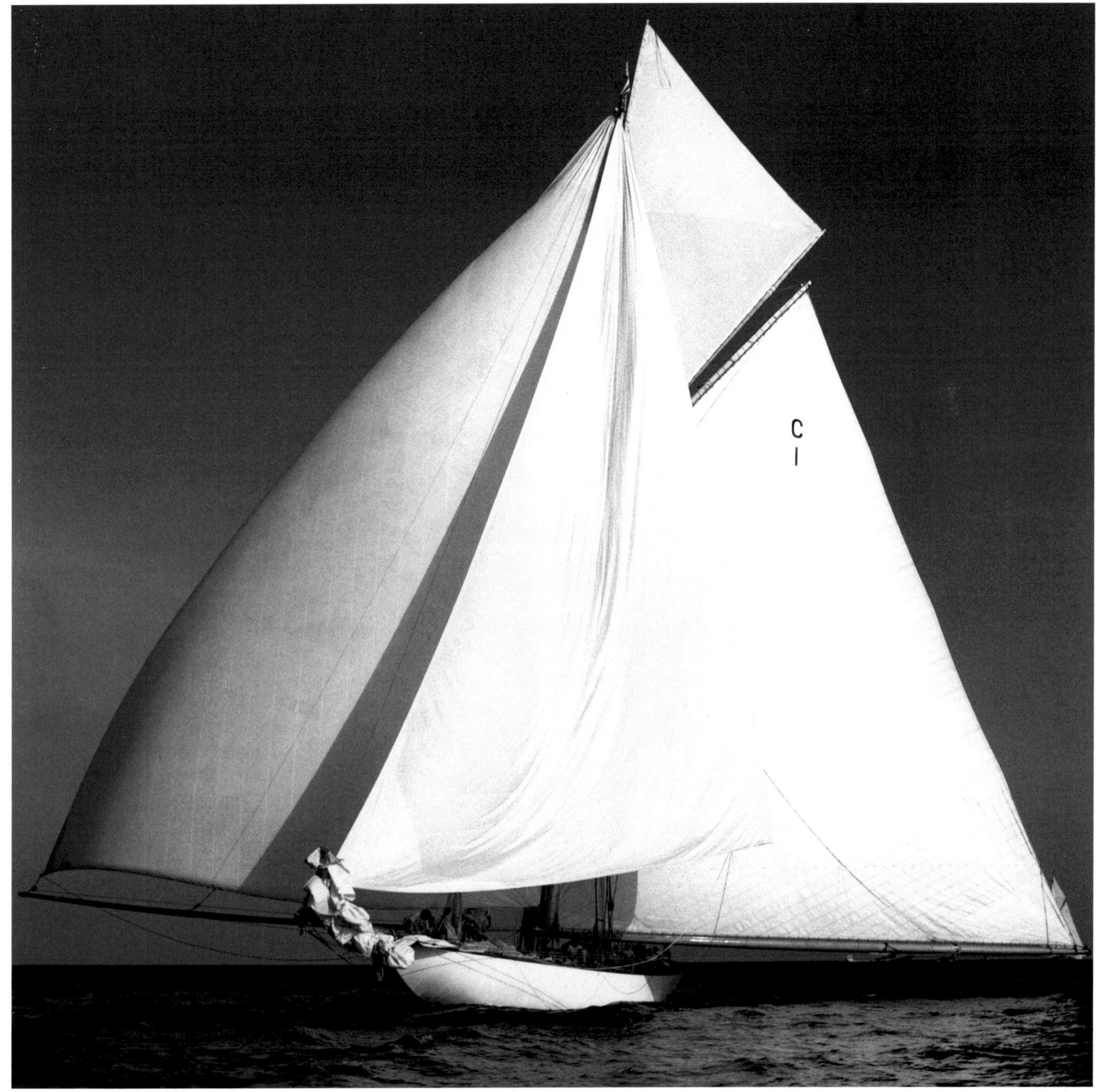

Mariquita, 2007

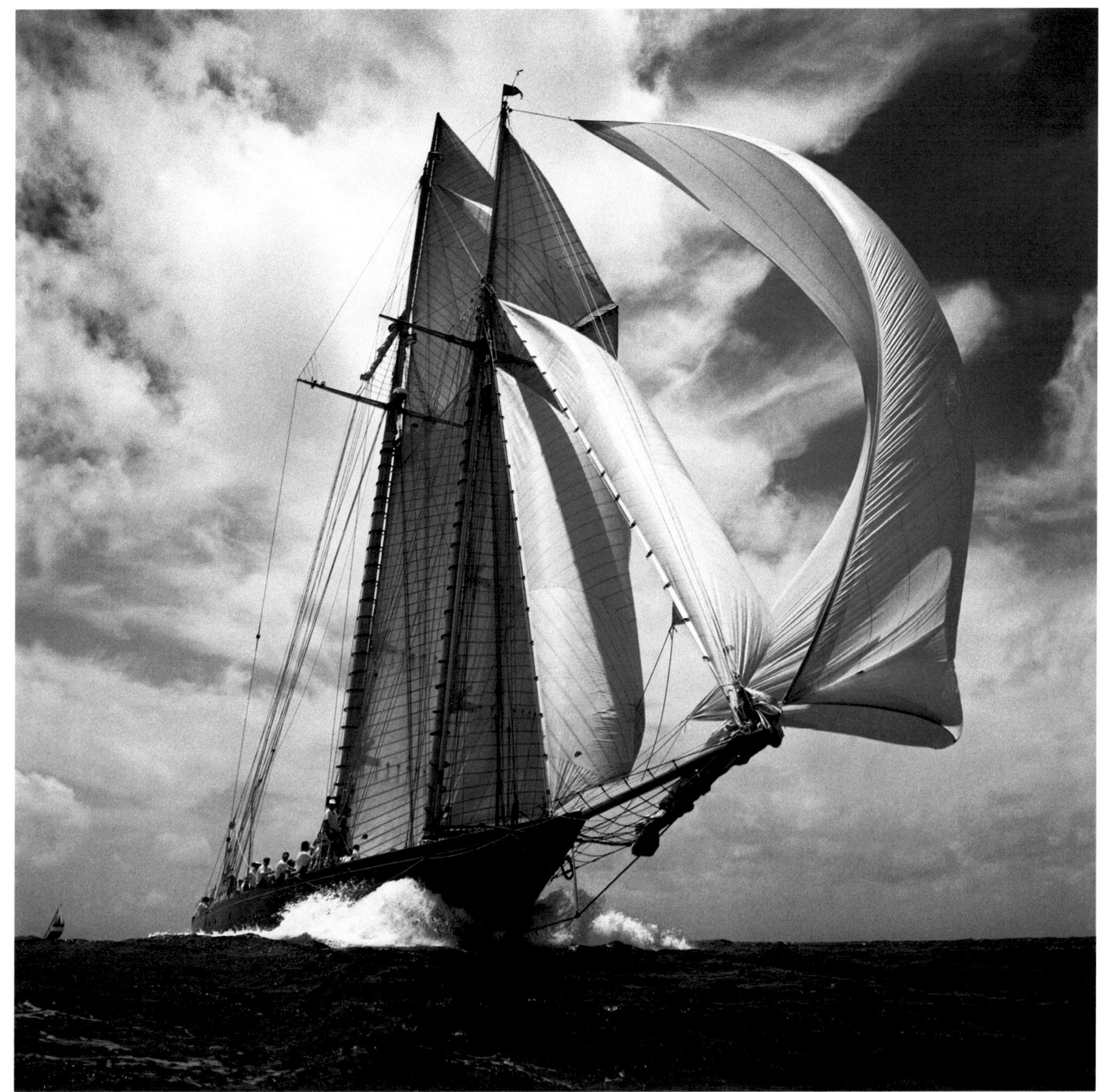

Marlette, 2000

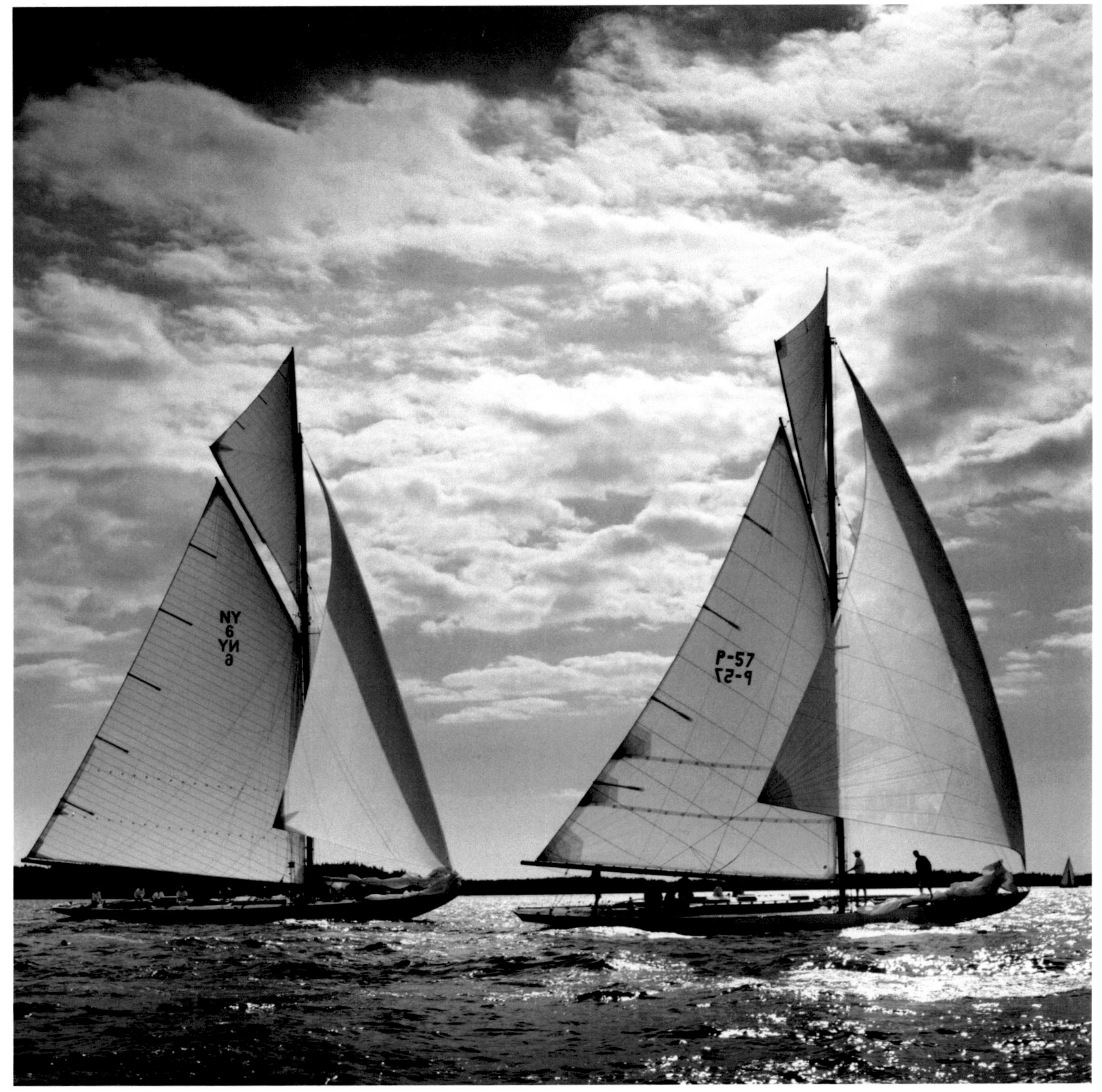

Spartan vs. Joyant, 2011

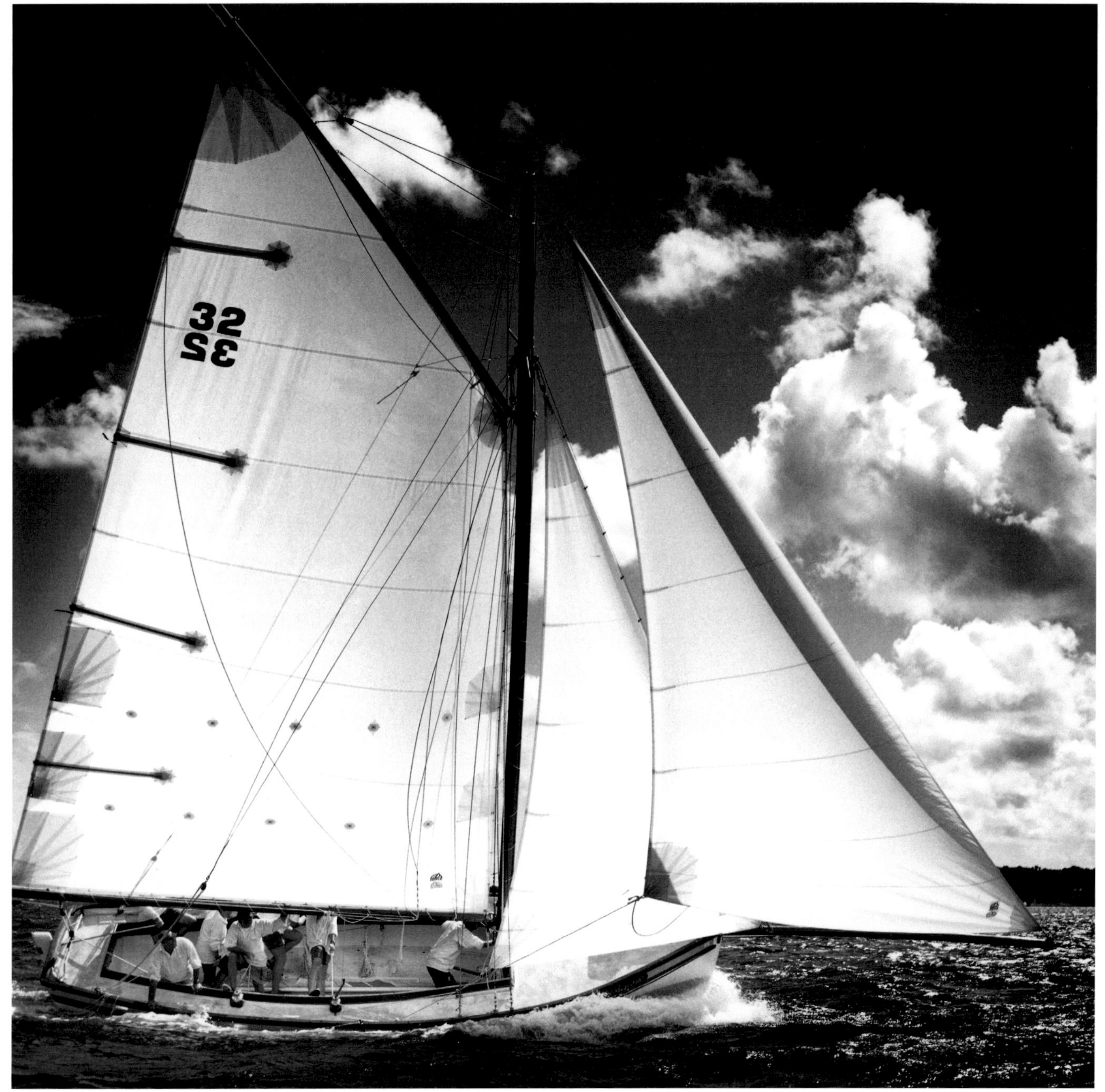

Abigail Rose, 2001

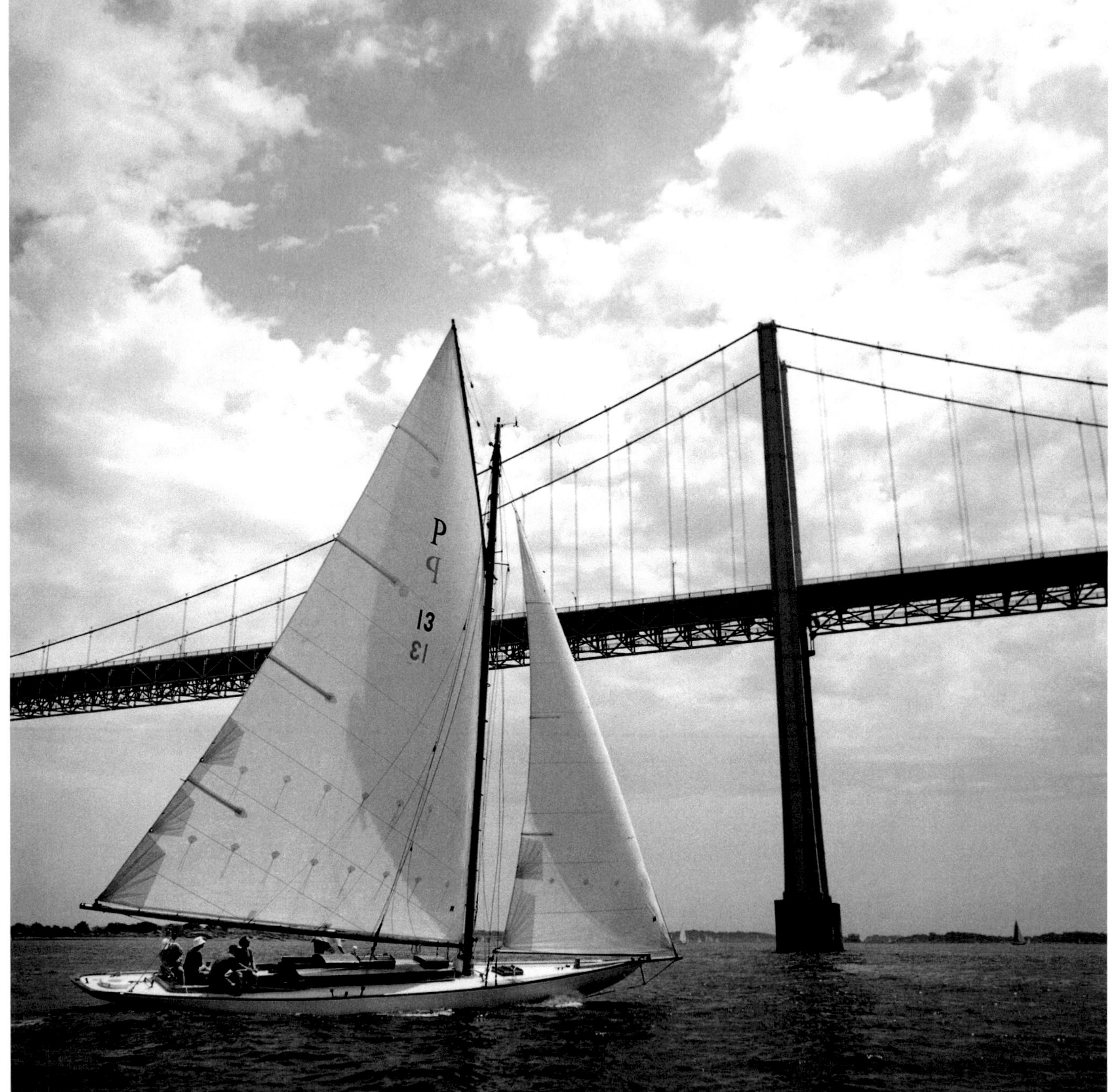

Chips, 2003

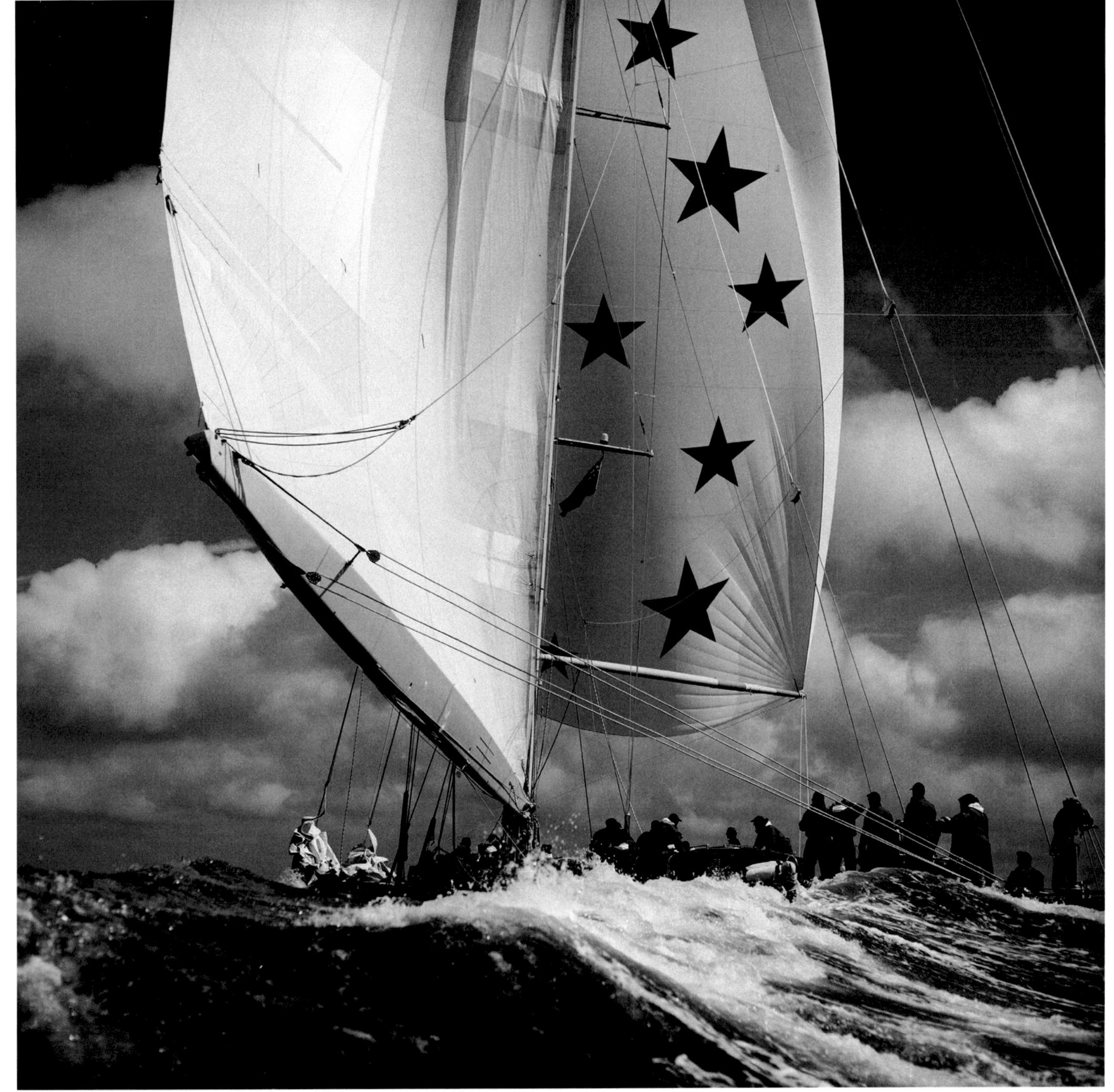

Endeavour, 2001

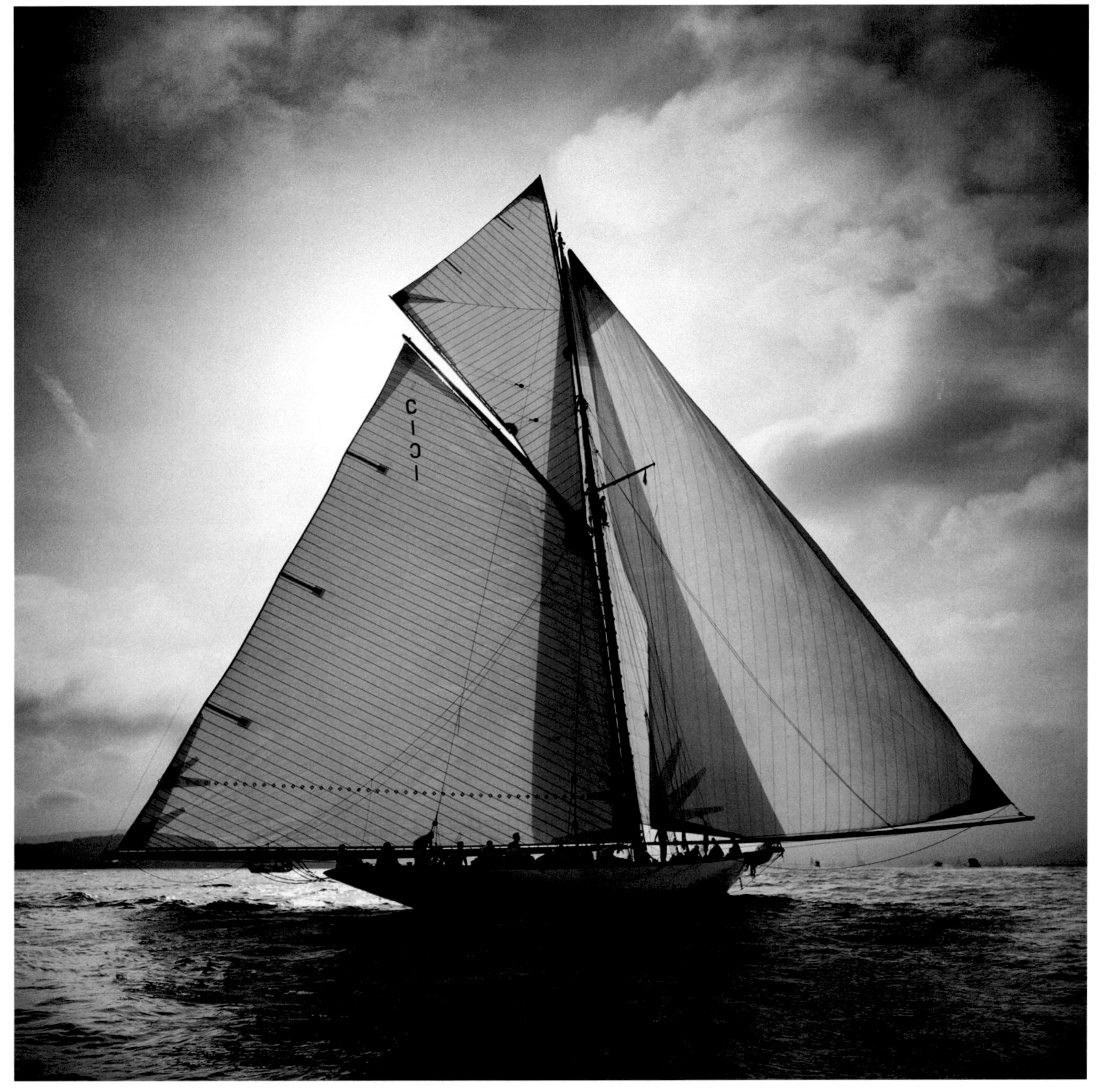

Mariquita, 2007

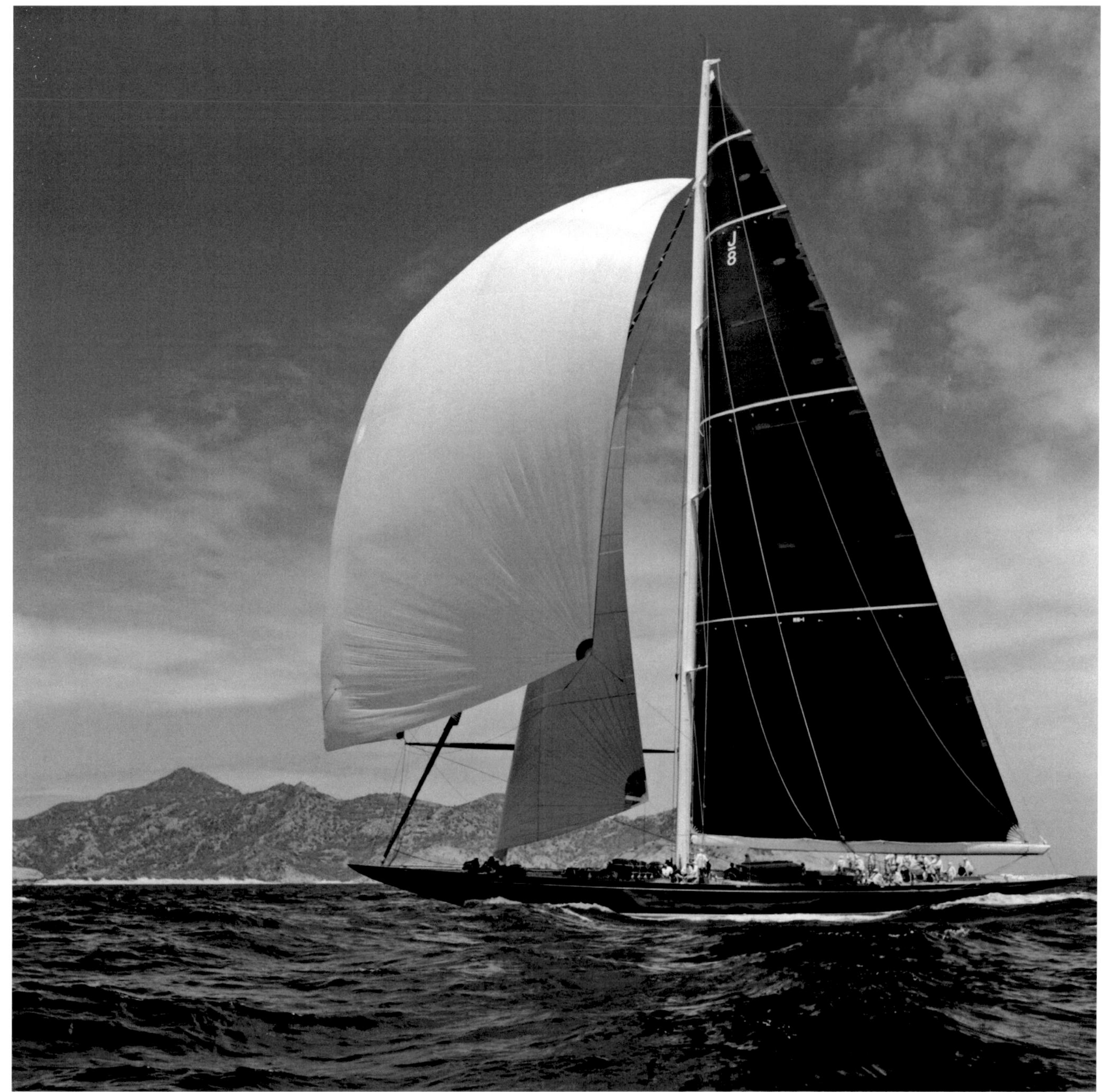

Topaz, 2017

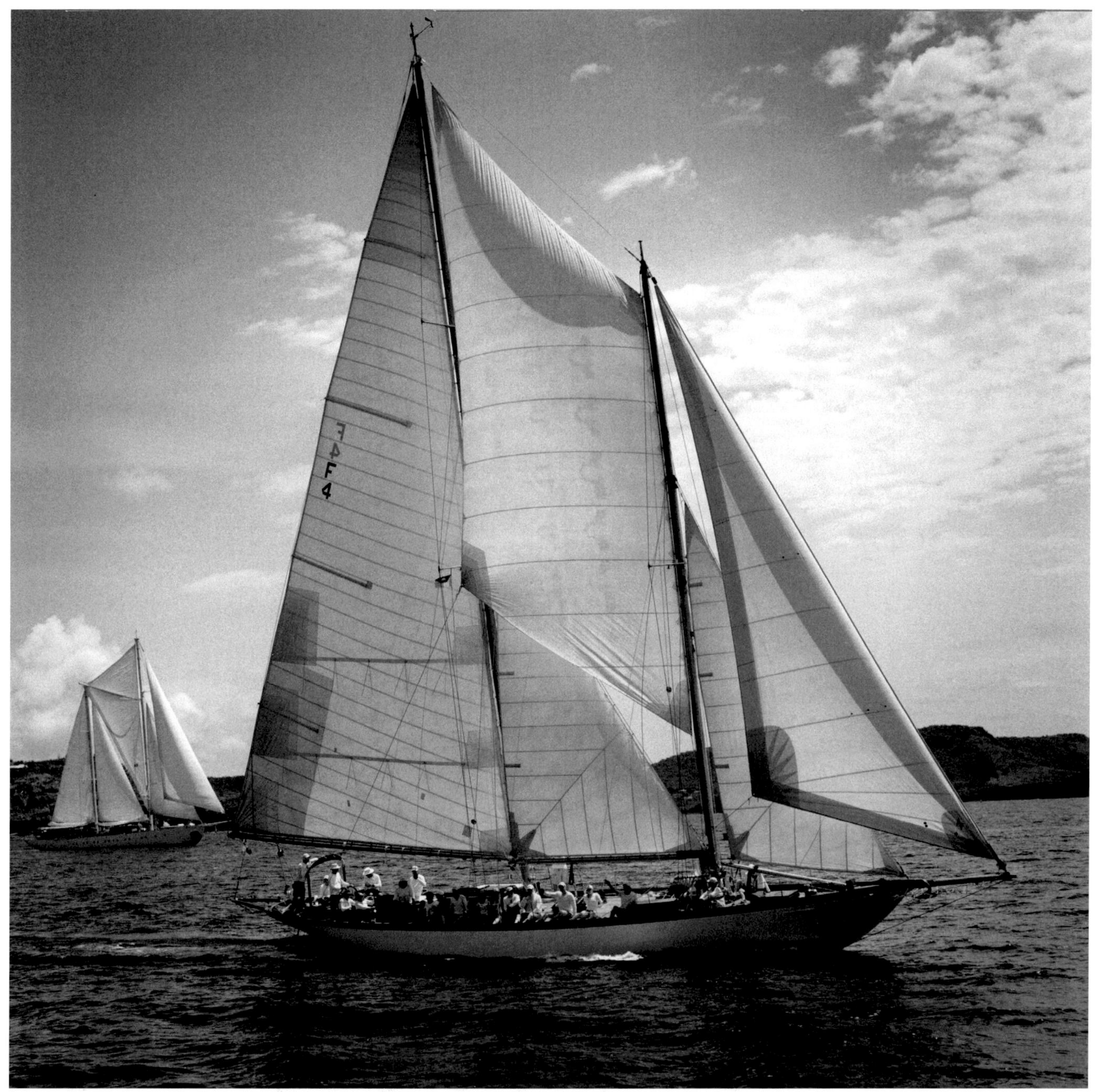

Mary Rose, 2016

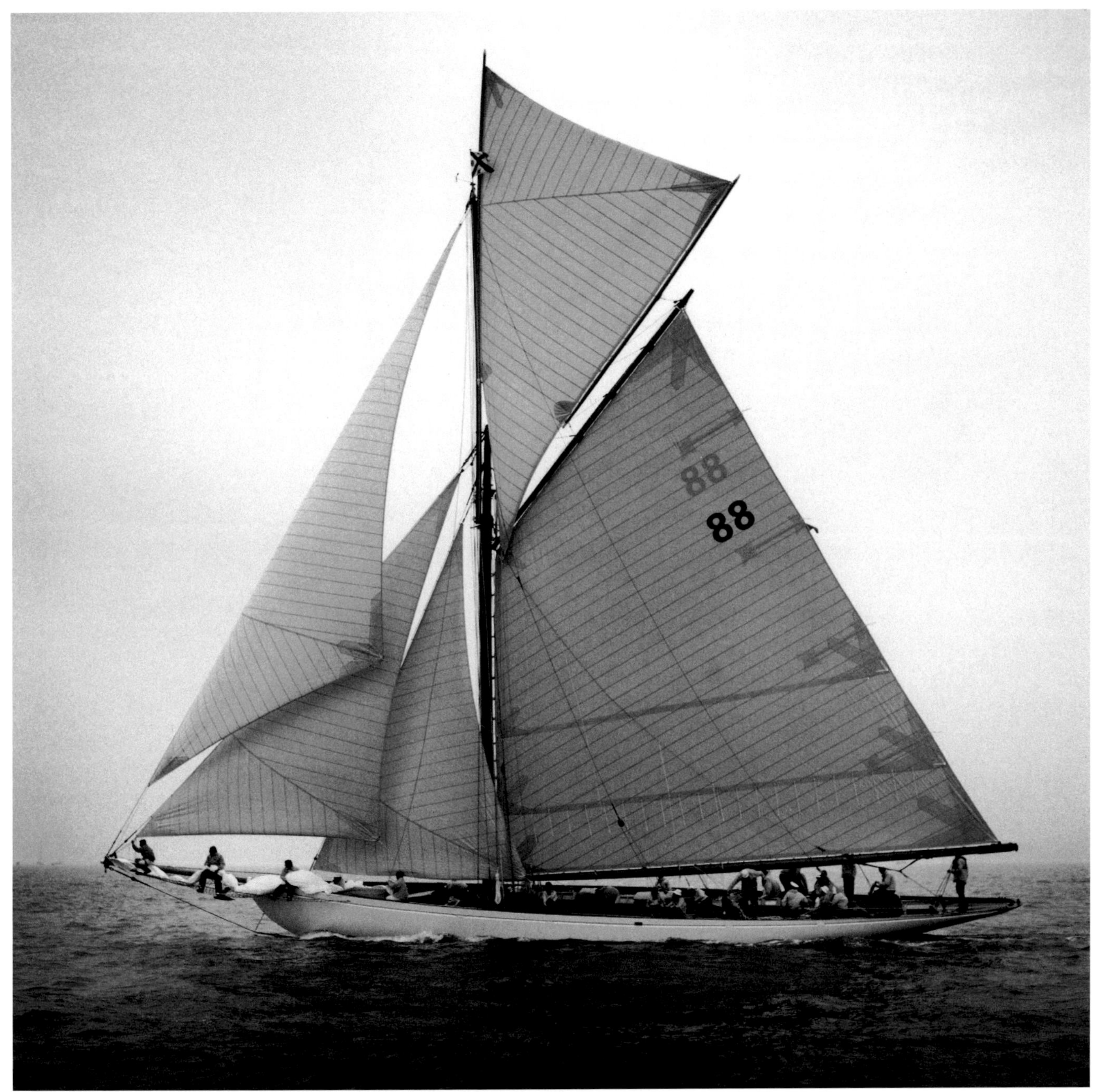

Moonbeam of Fife, 2001

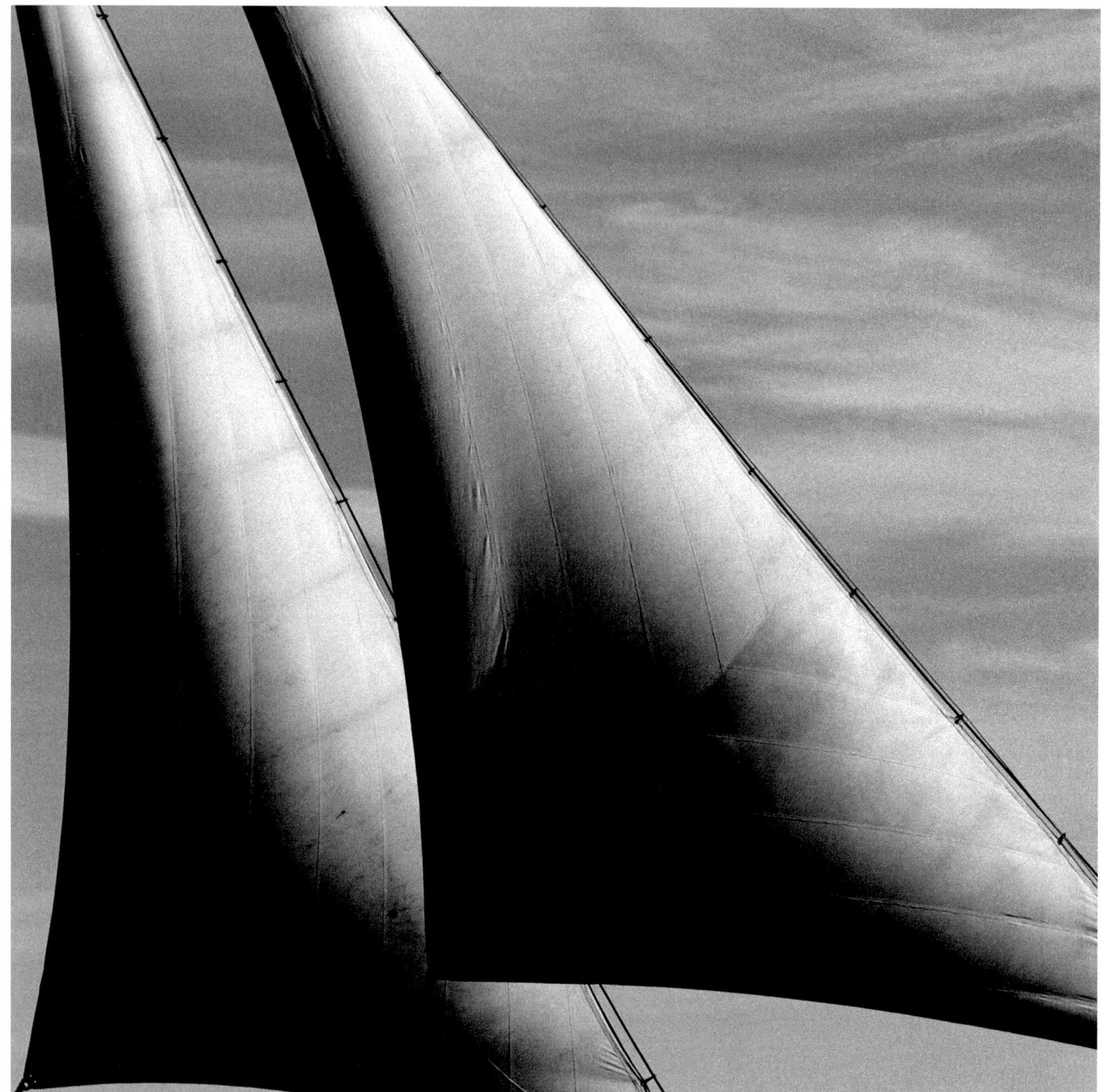

J&E Riggin, 1999

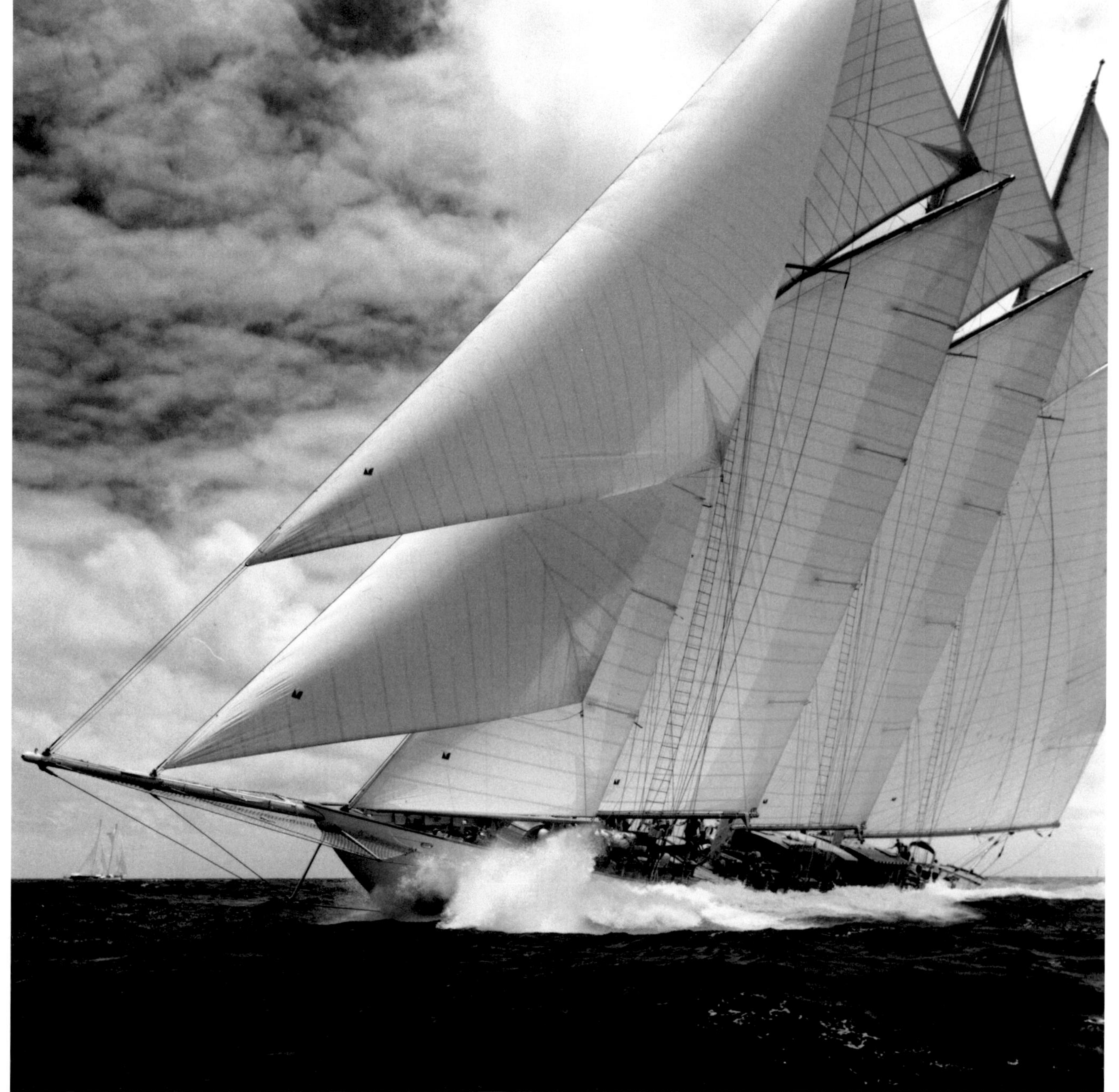

Adix, 2017

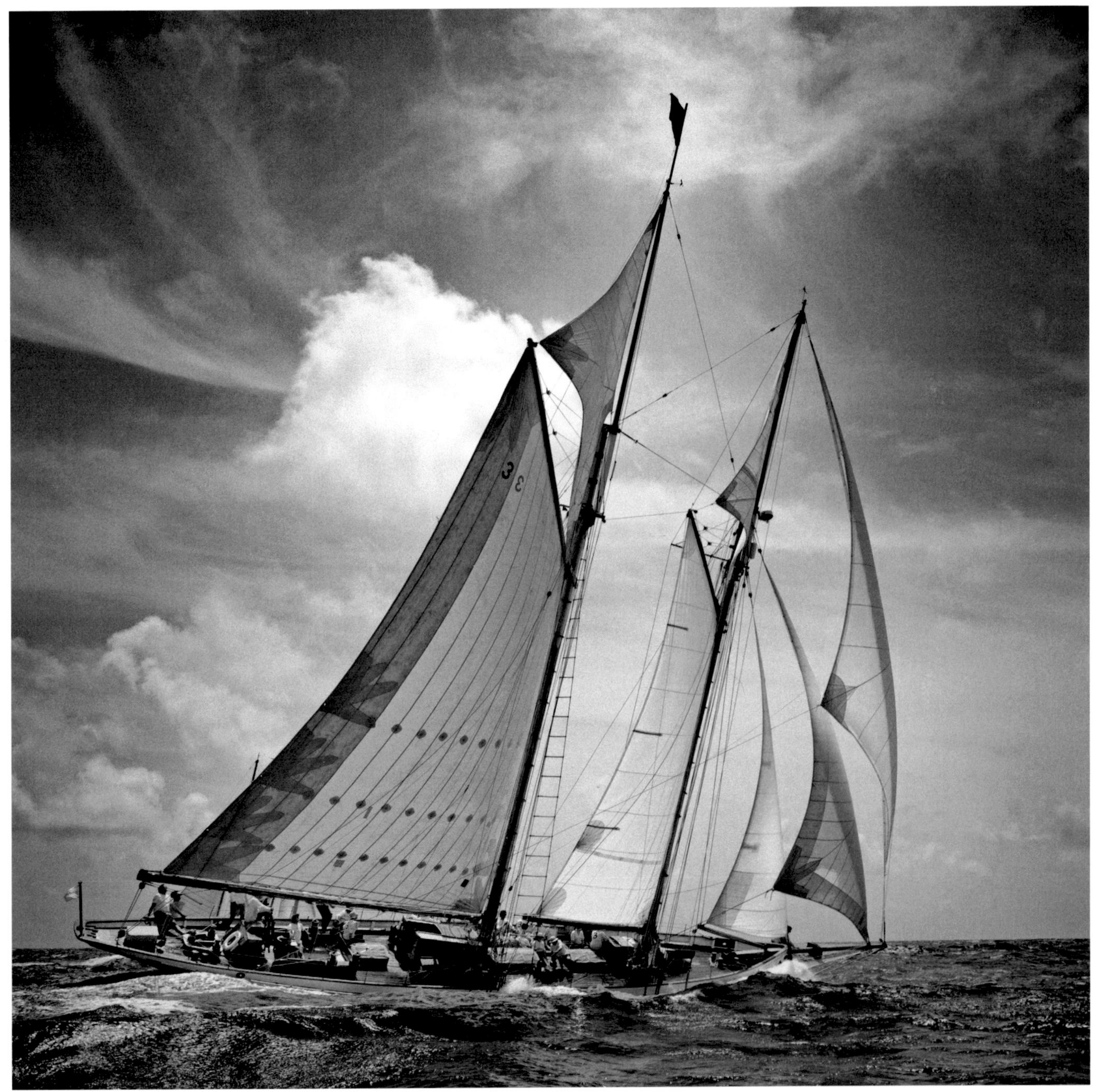

Coral of Cowes, 2015

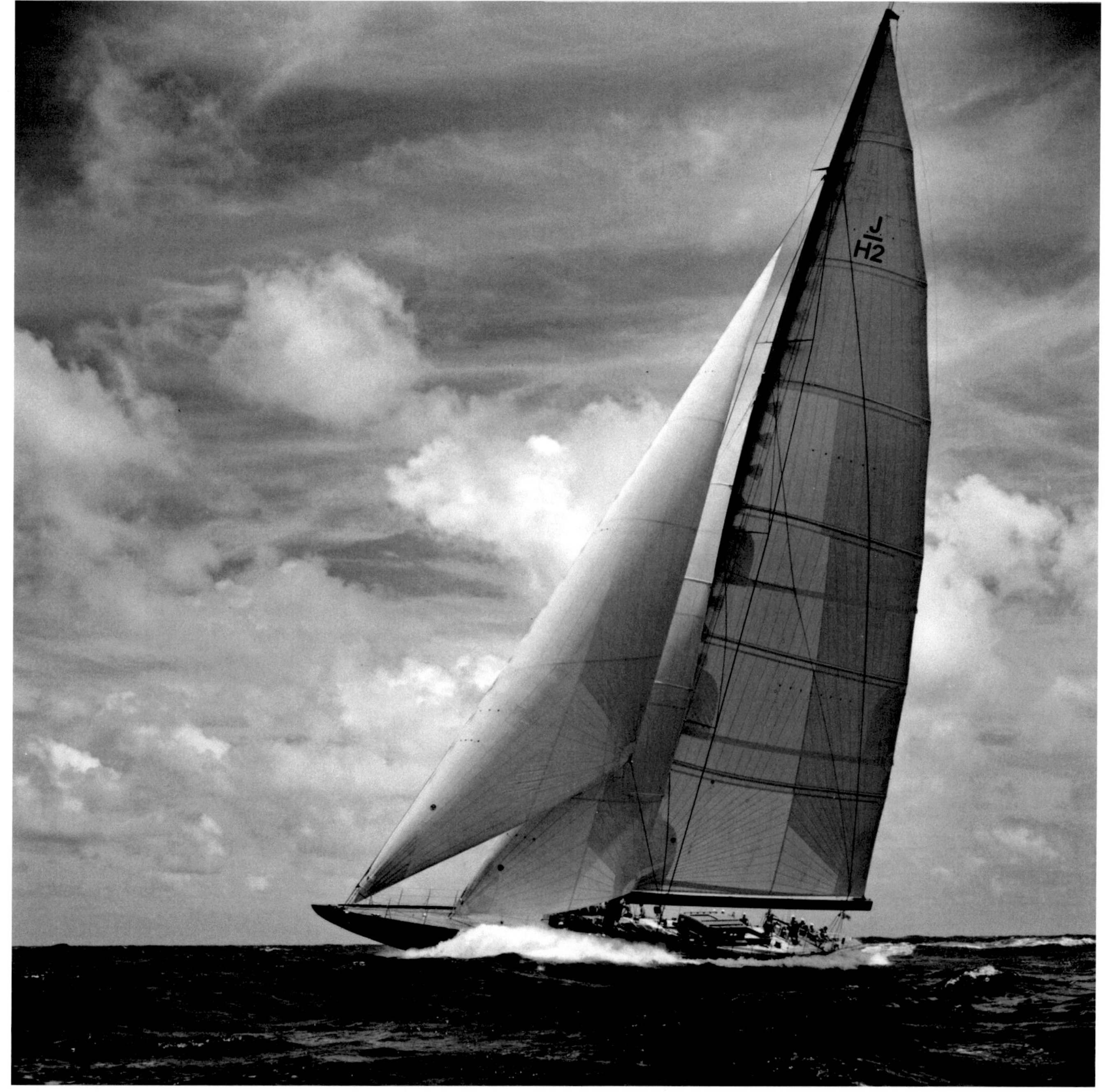

Rainbow, 2015

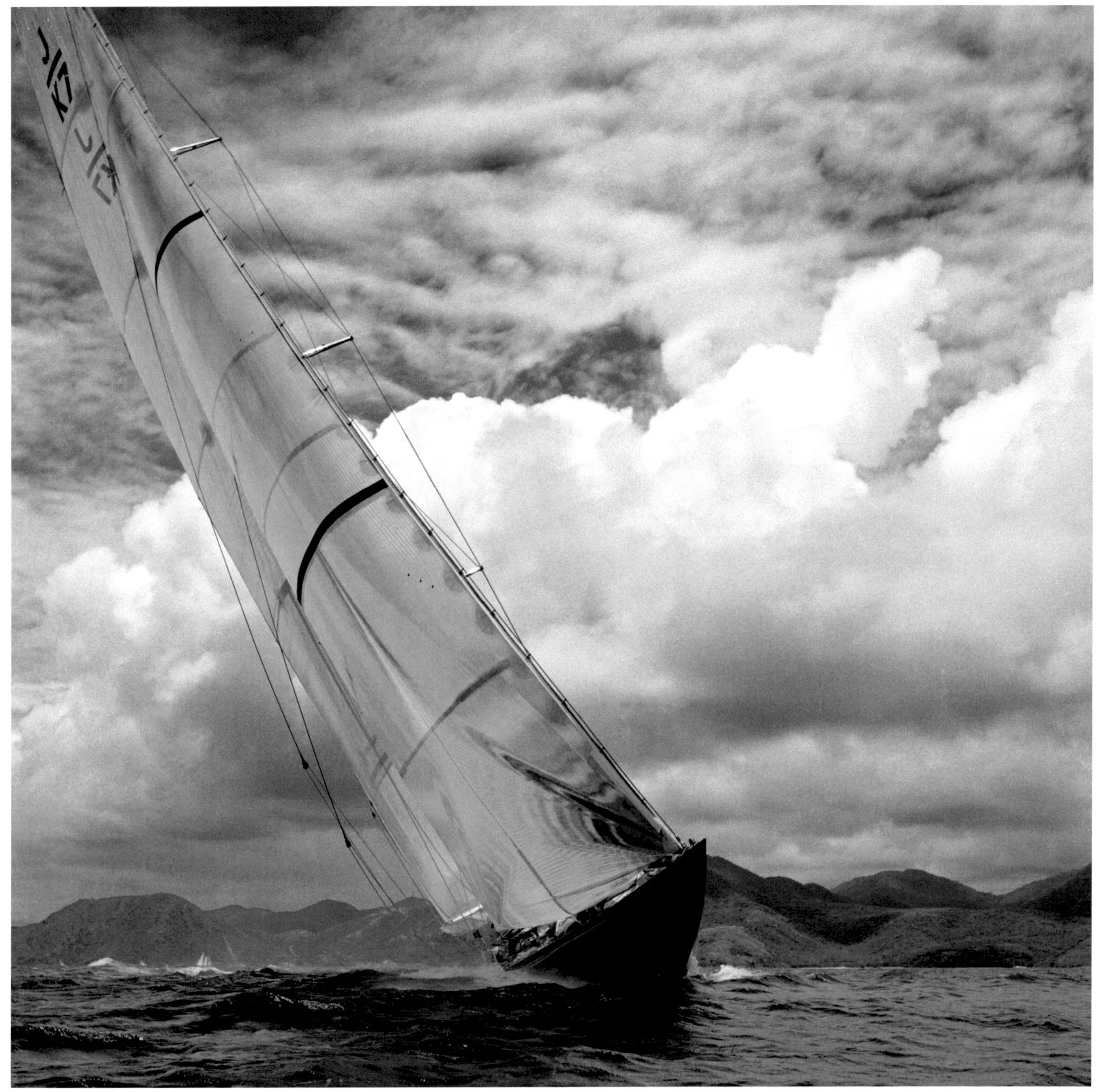

Velsheda, 2004

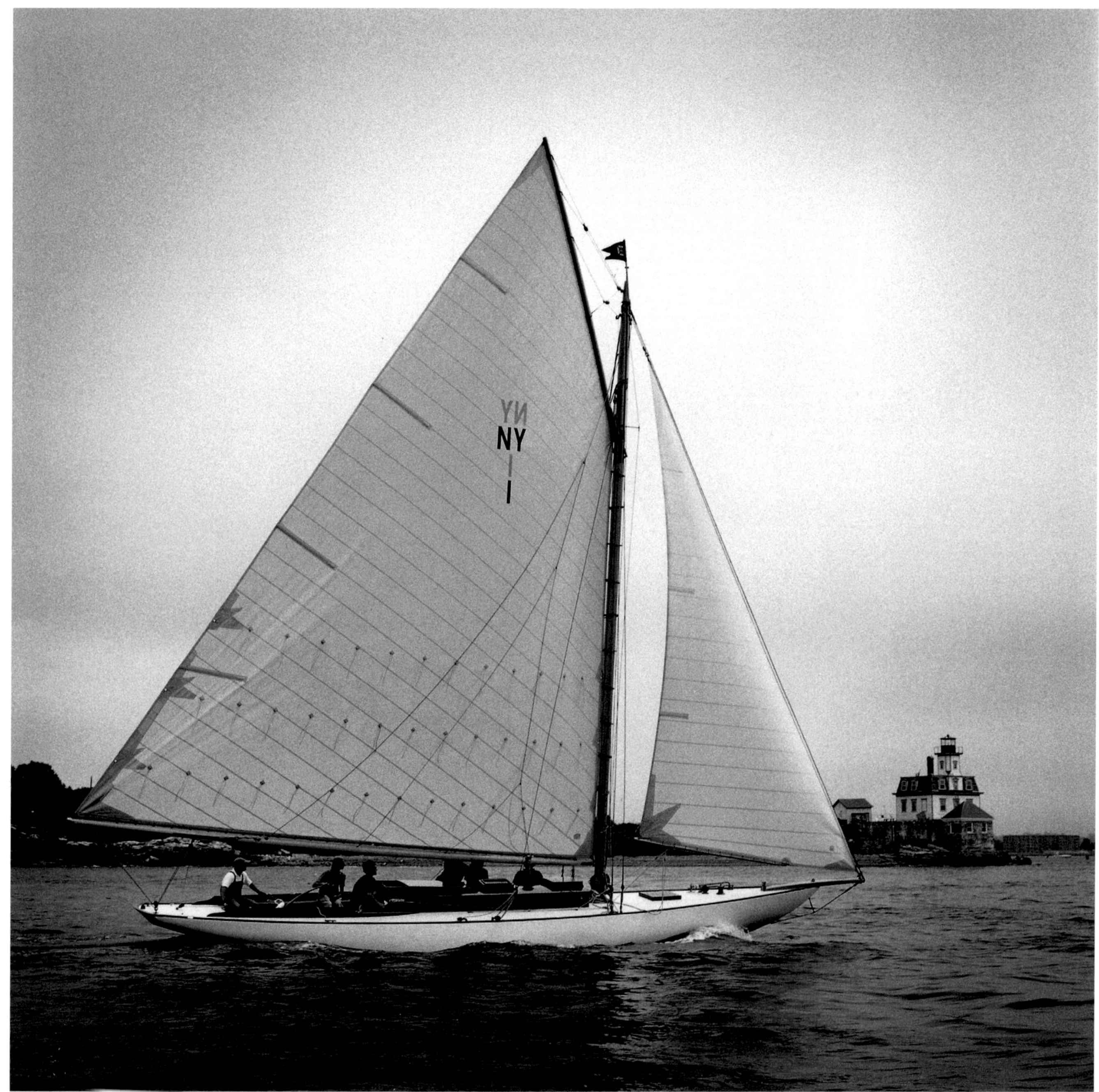

Alera, 2005

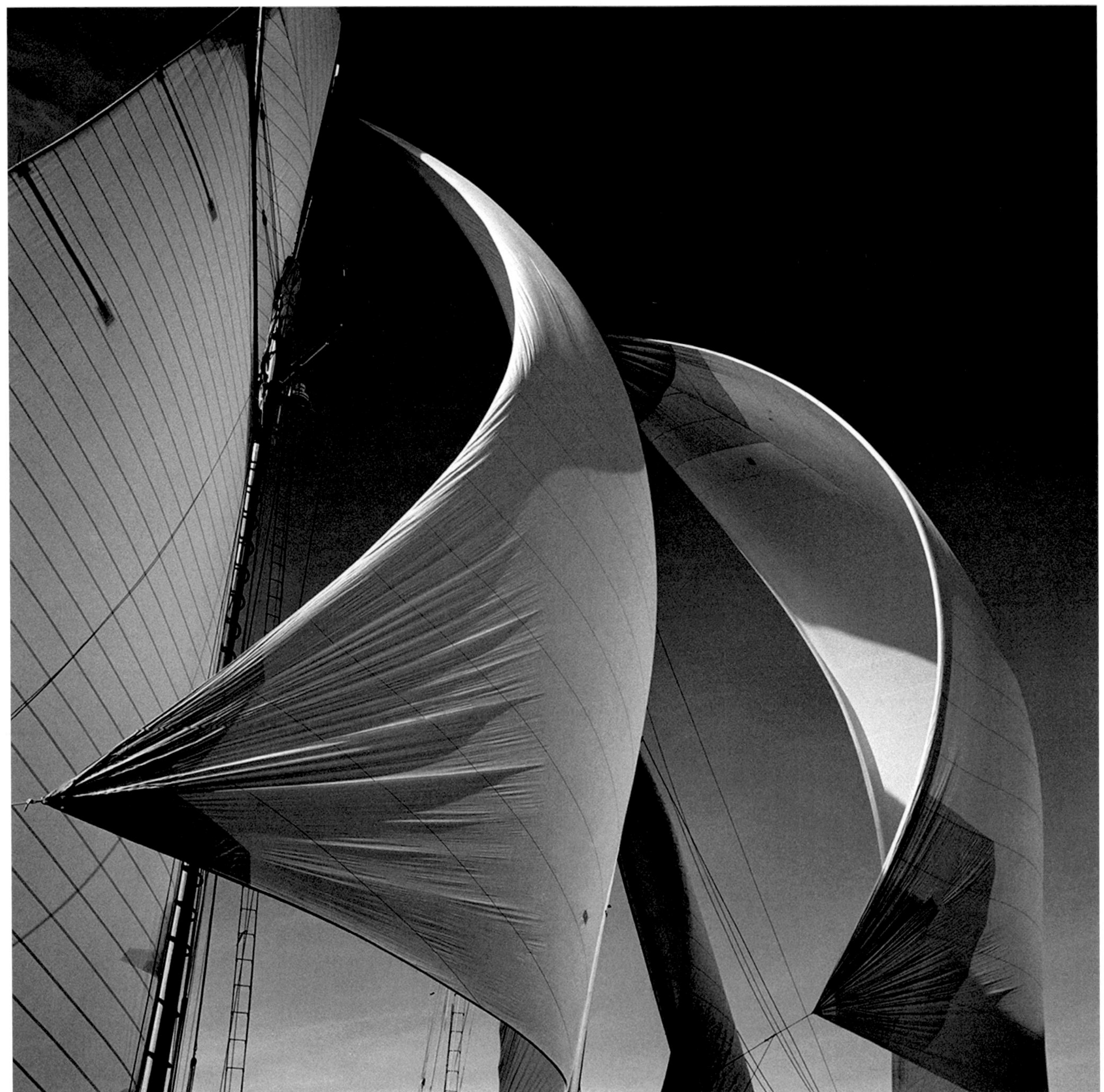

Mariette, 2008

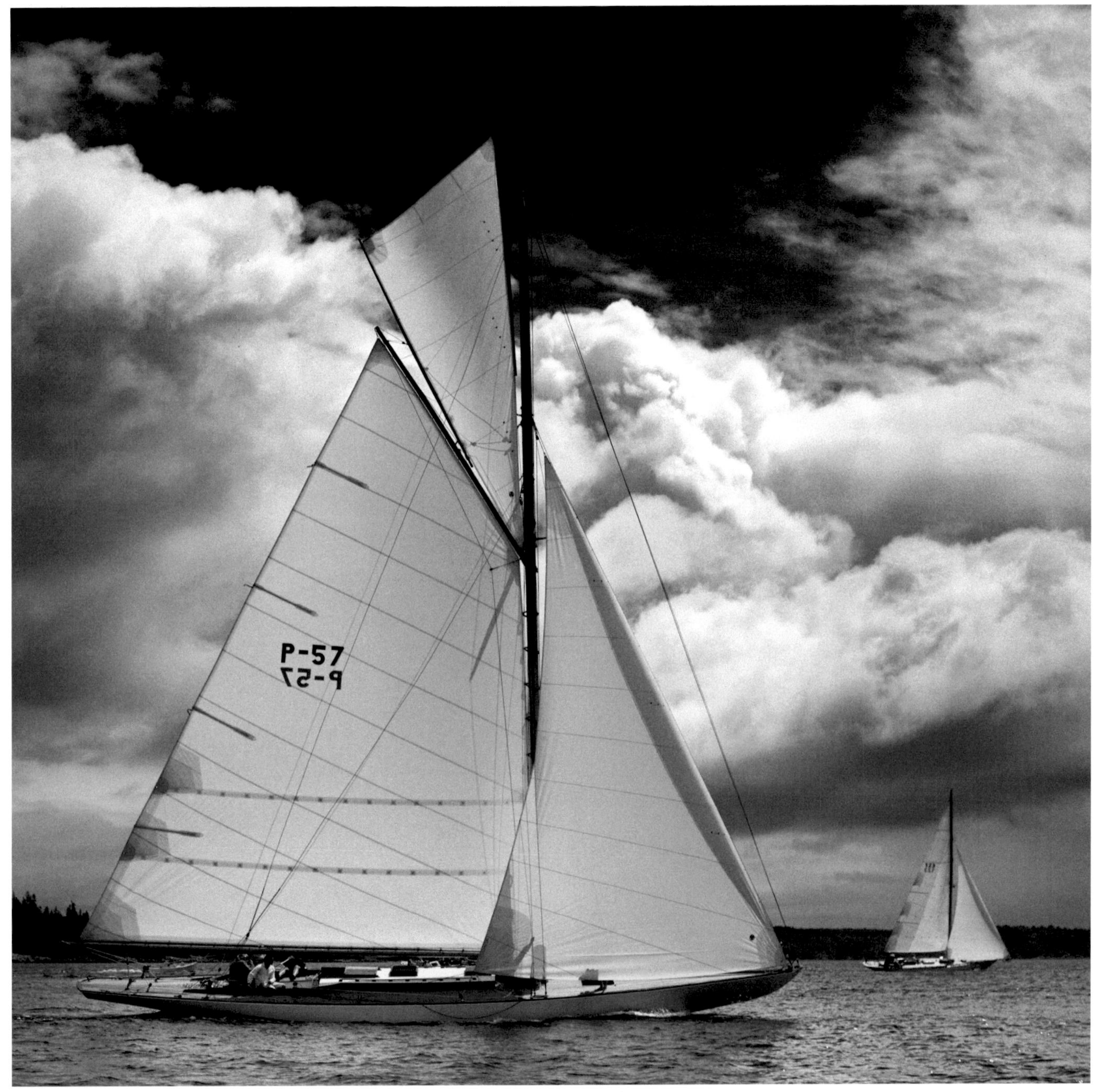

Joyant, 2011

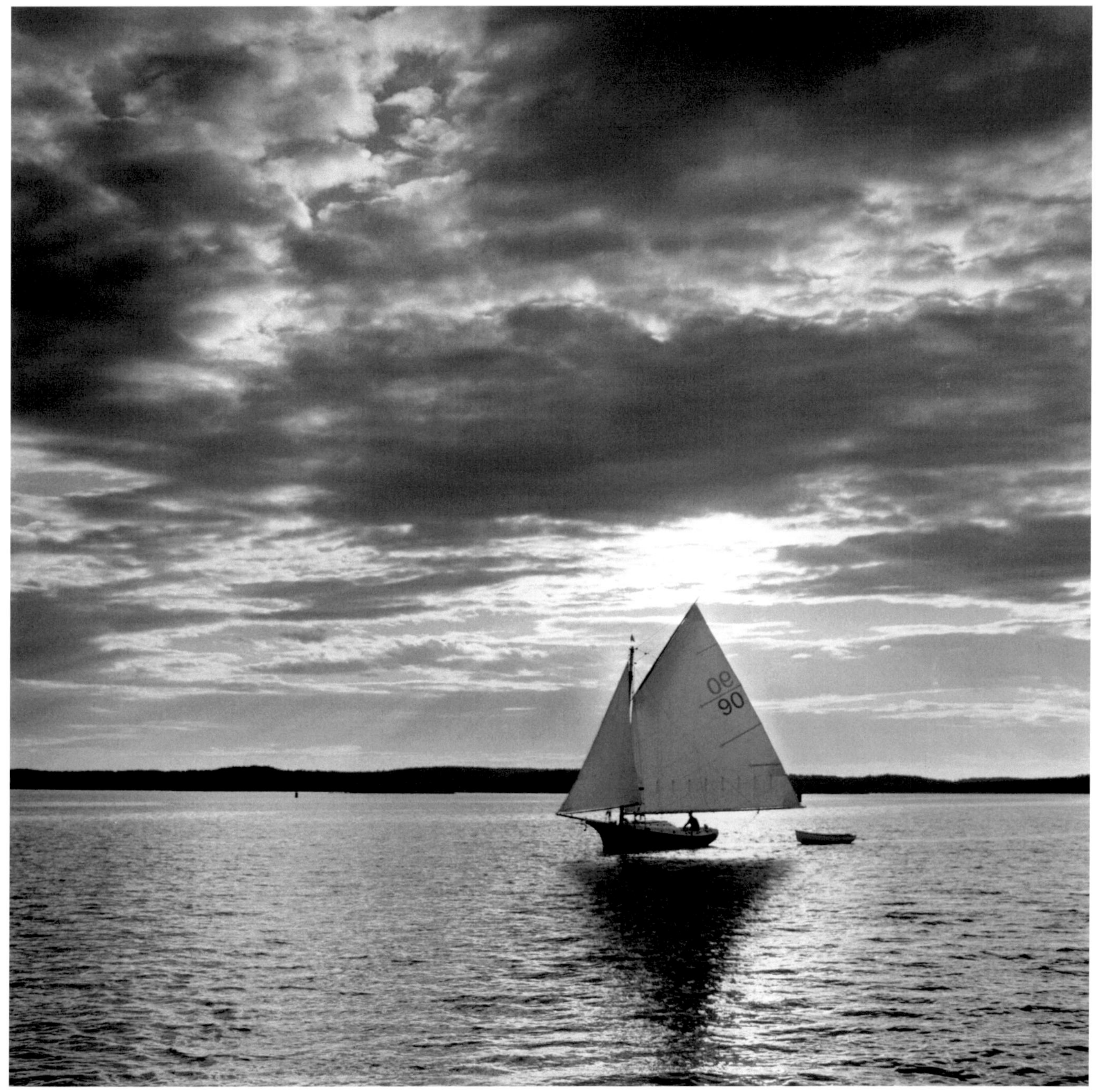

Salatia, 2010

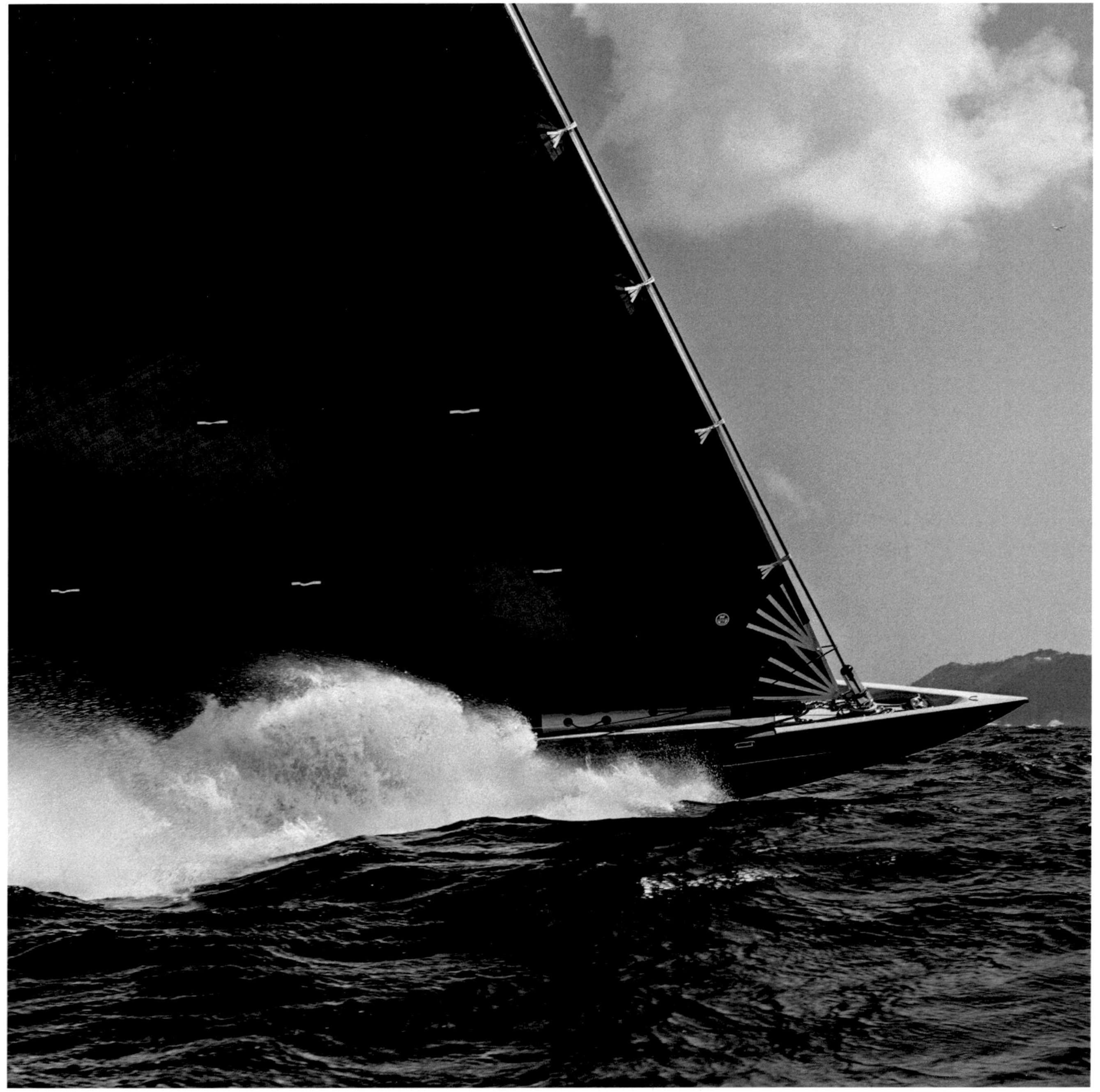

Topaz, 2017

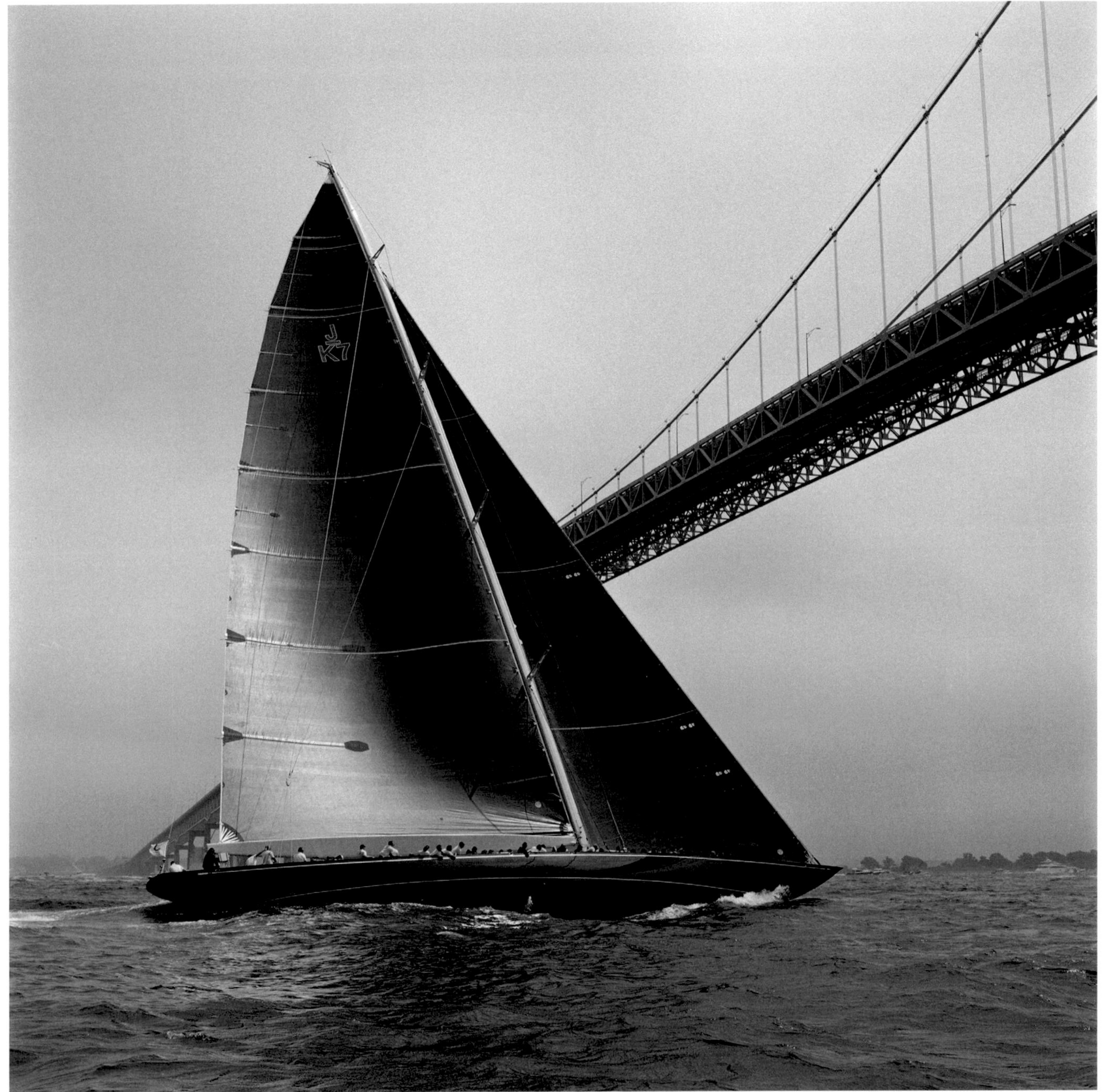

Velsheda, 2017

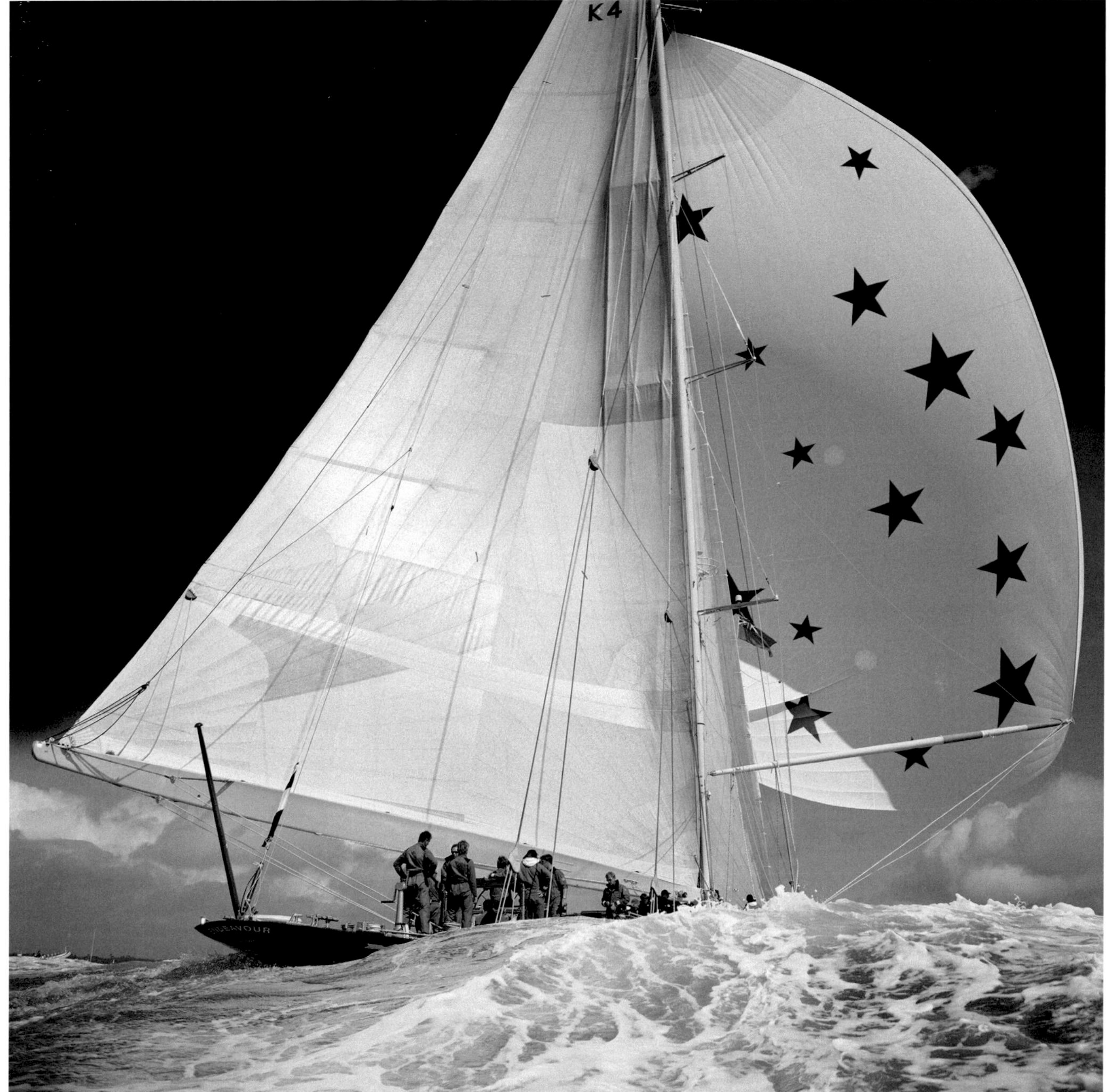

Endeavour, 2001

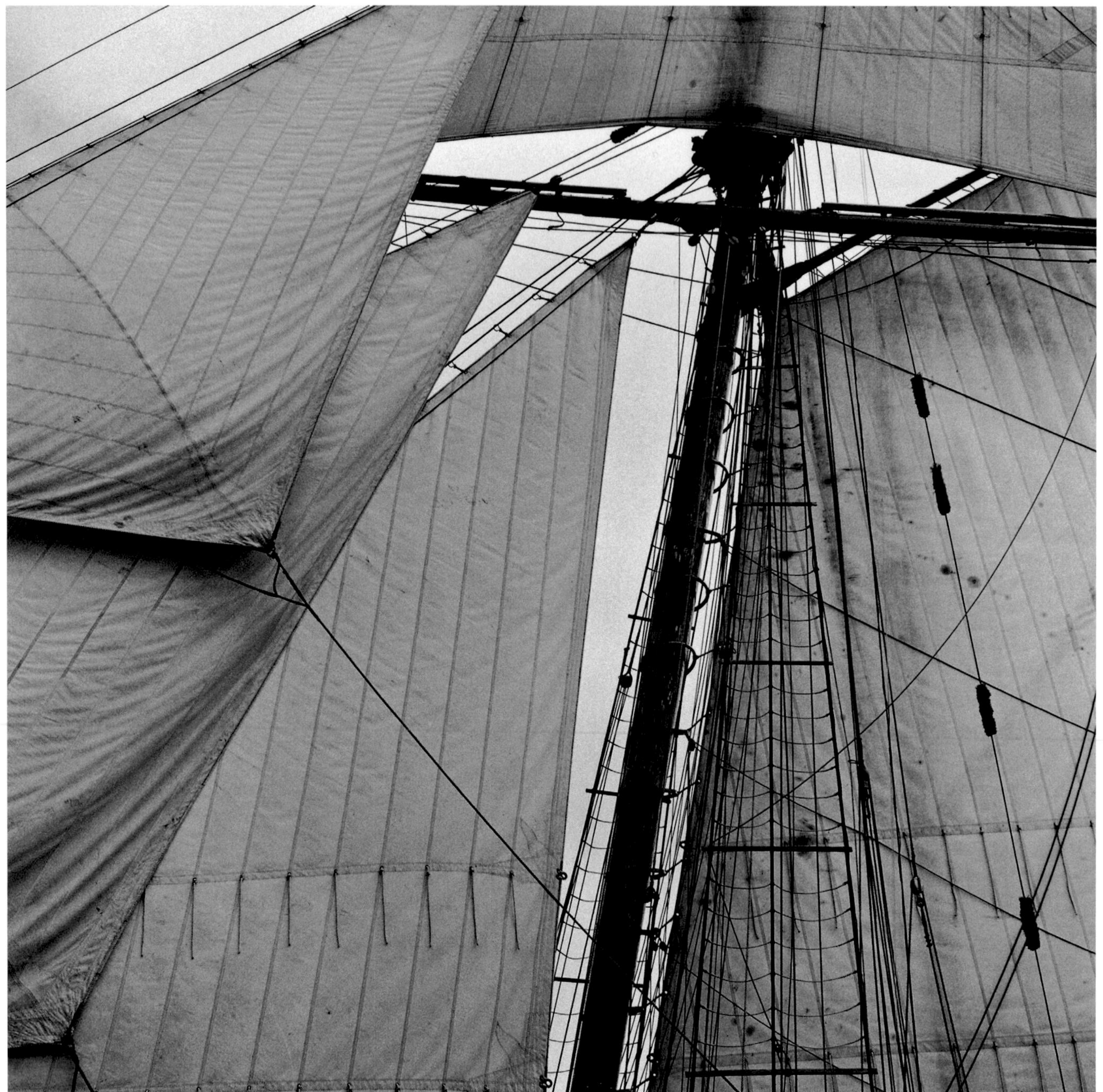

Pride of Baltimore, 2004

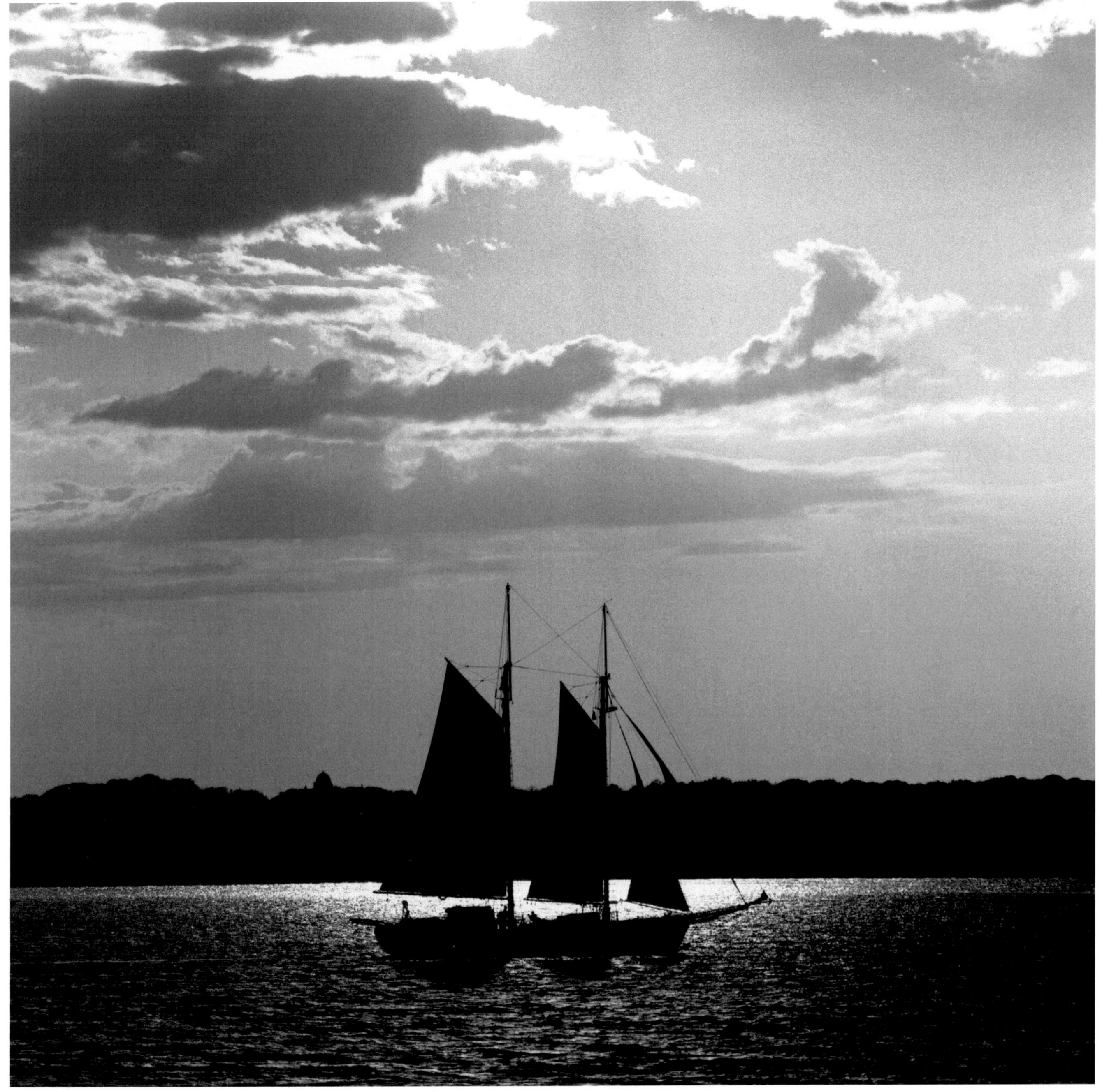

Madeleine, 2017

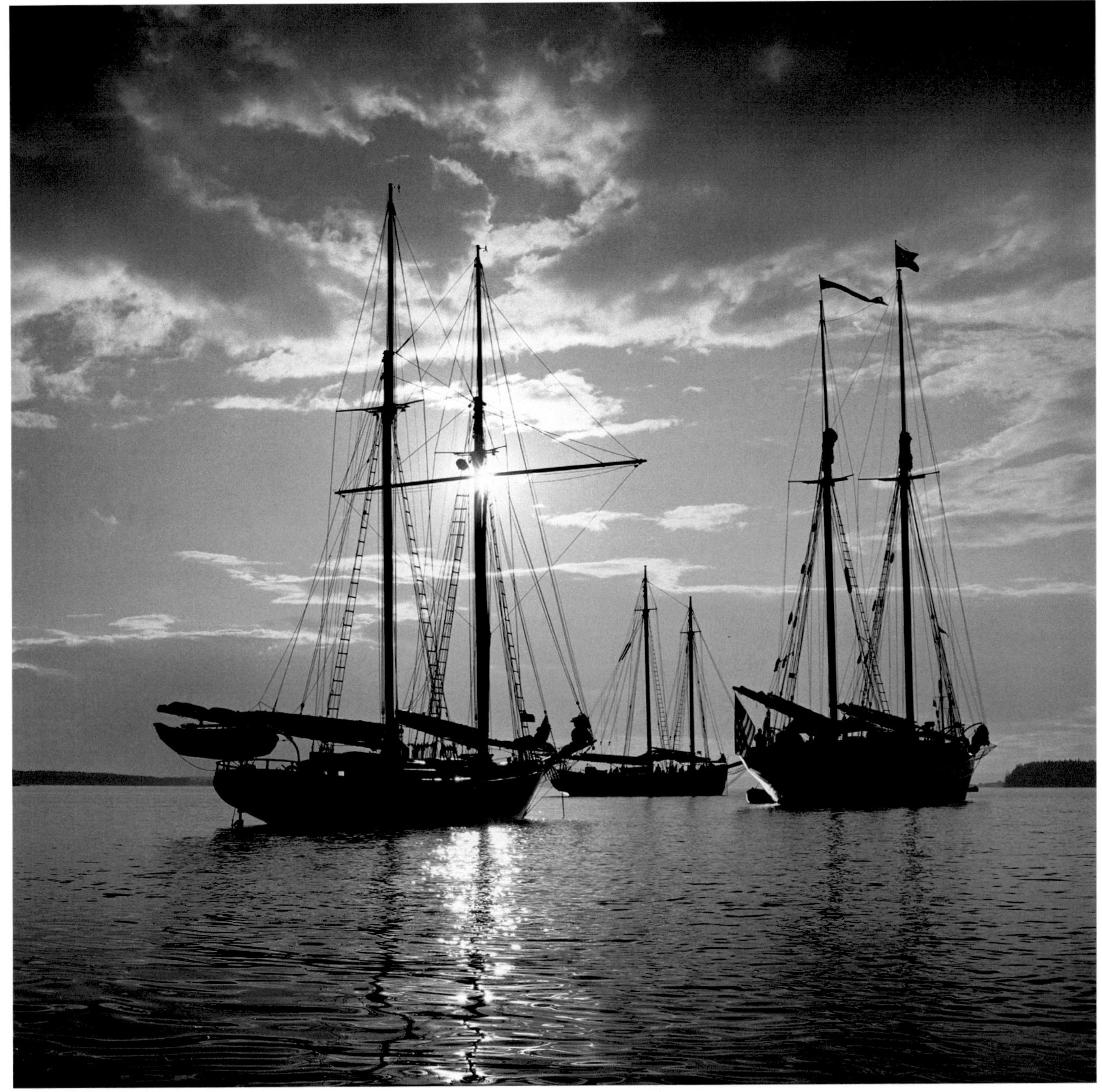

Moored Schooners, 2010

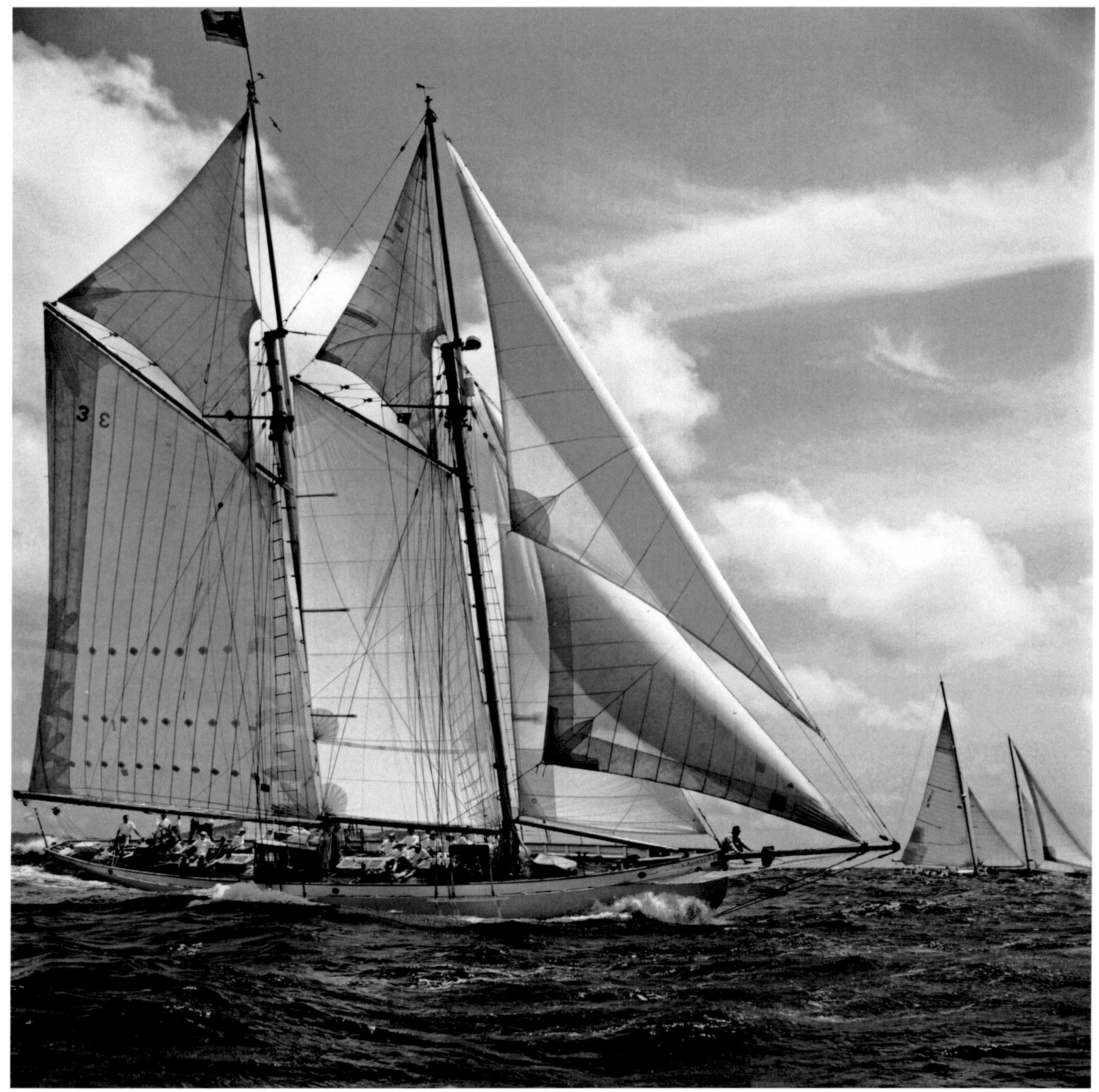

Coral of Cowes, 2015

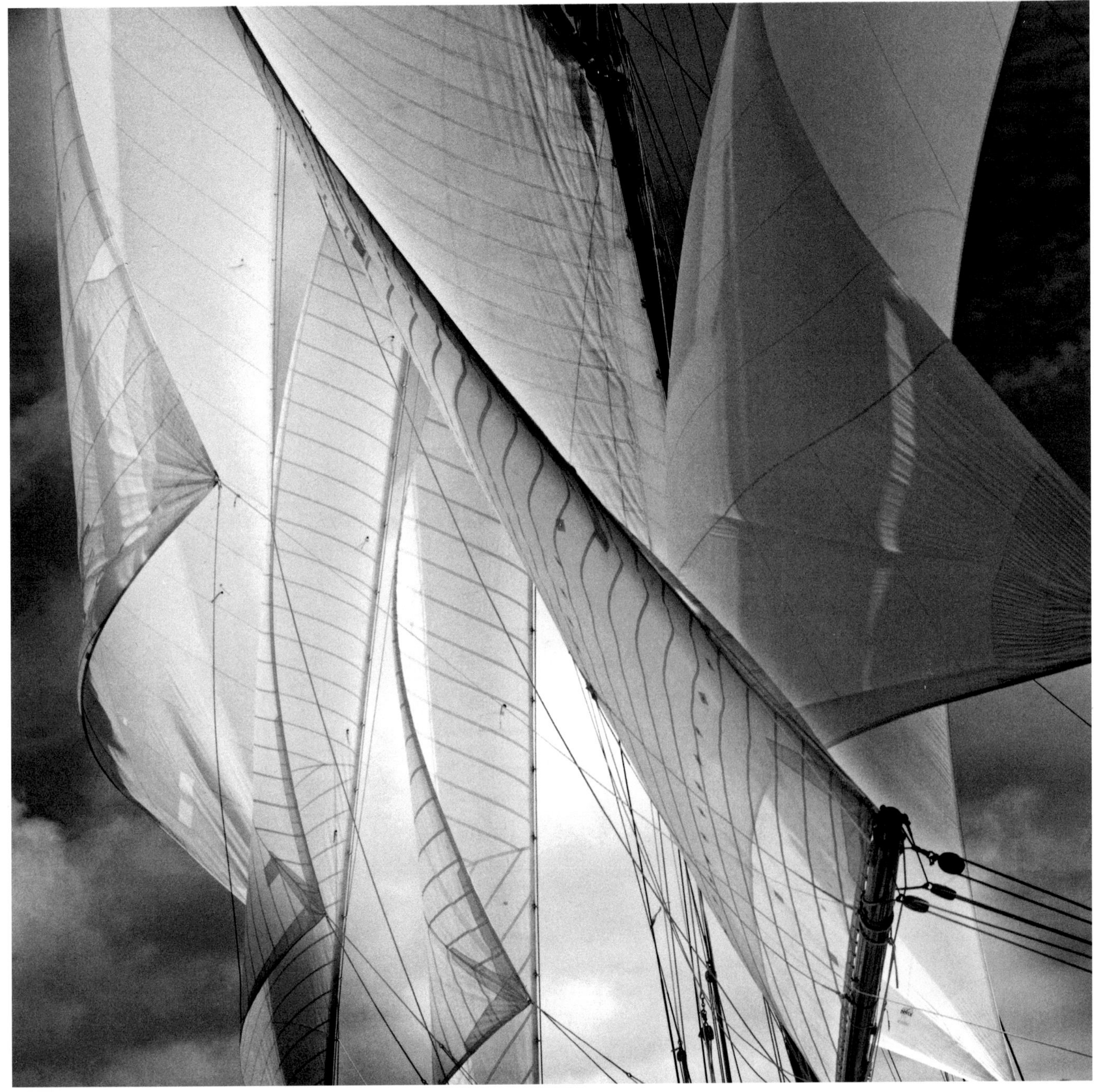

Sails of Thendara, 2001

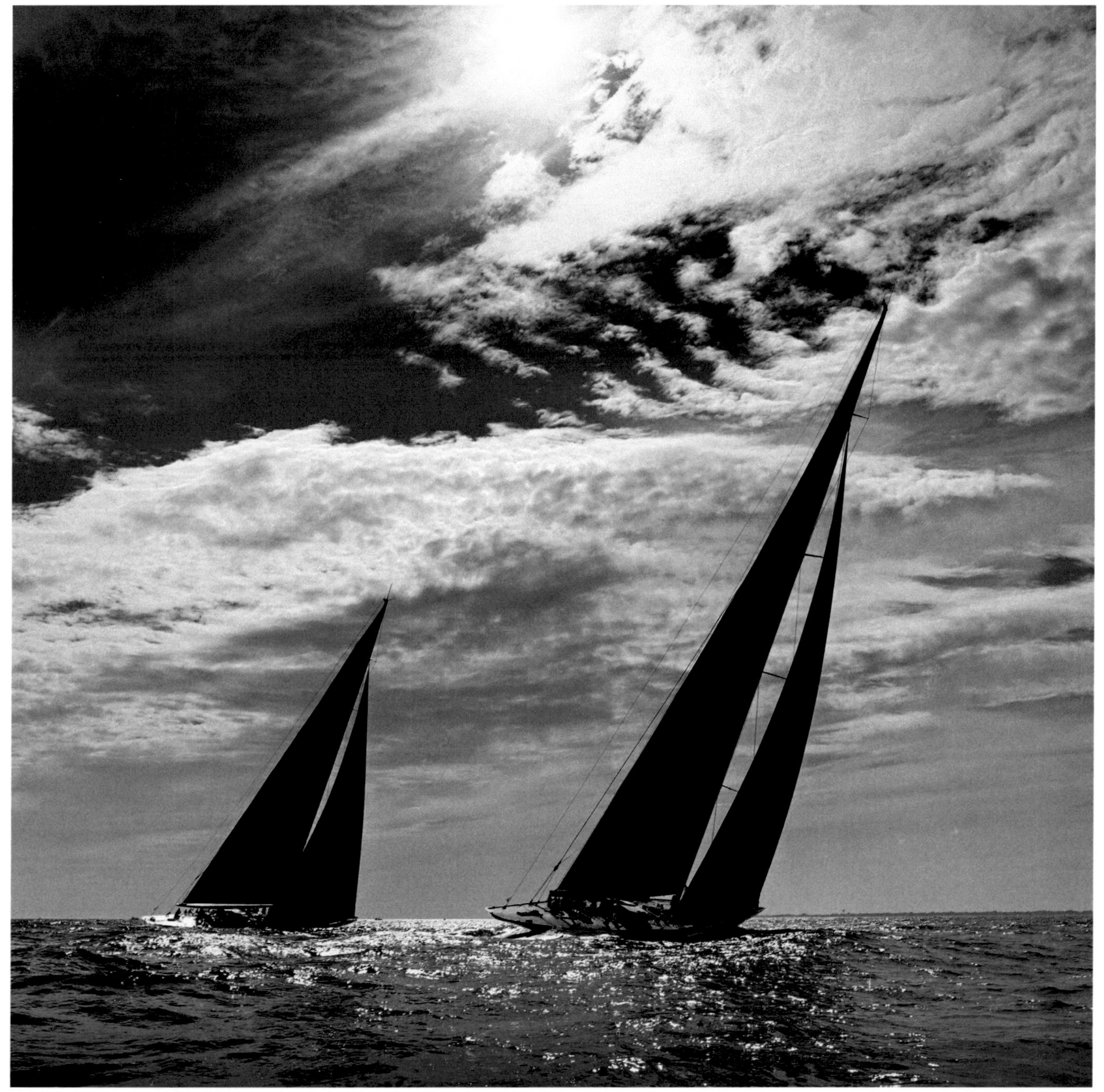

J Class Racing, 2017

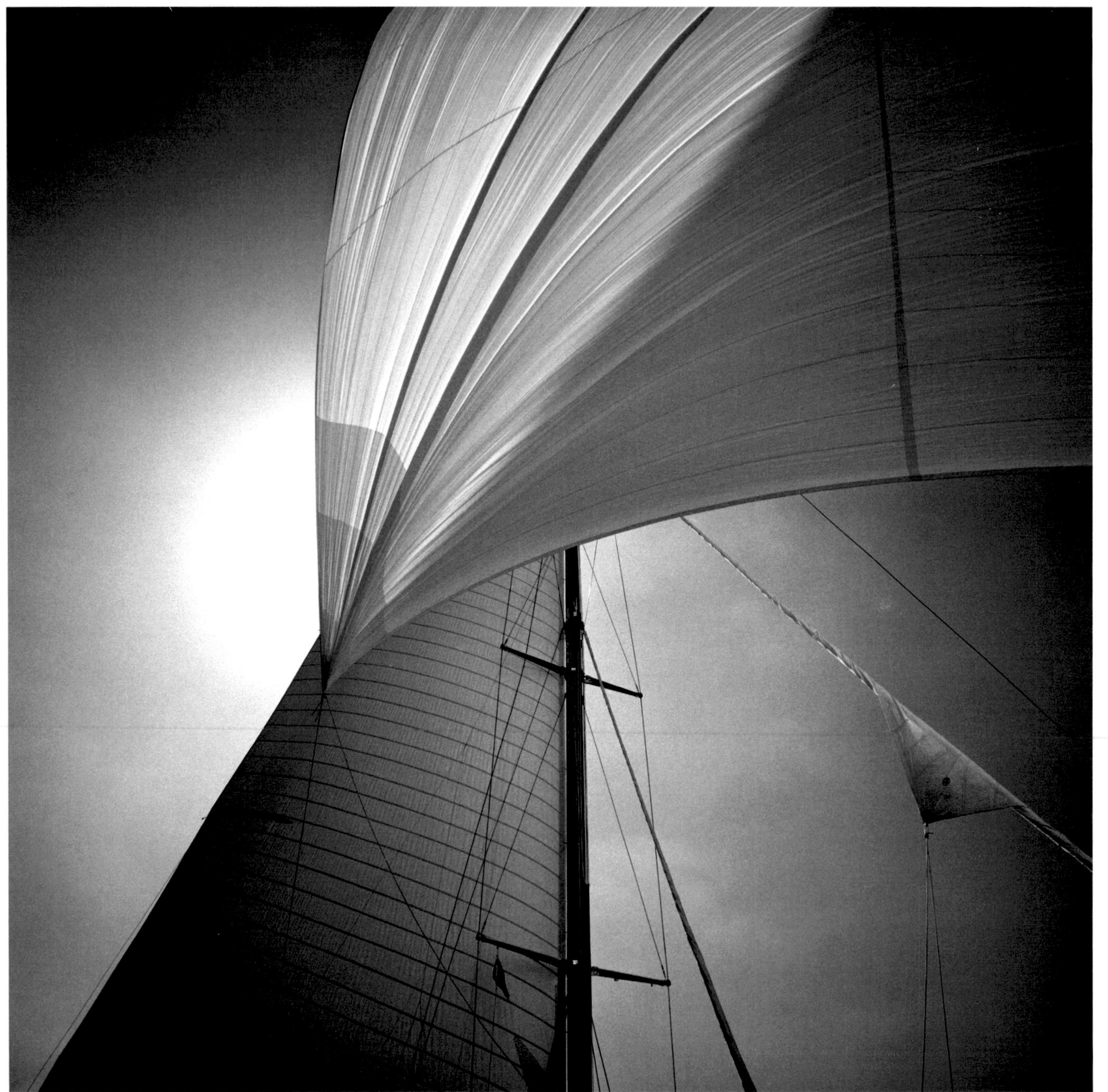

Spinnaker Detail of Cambria, 2001

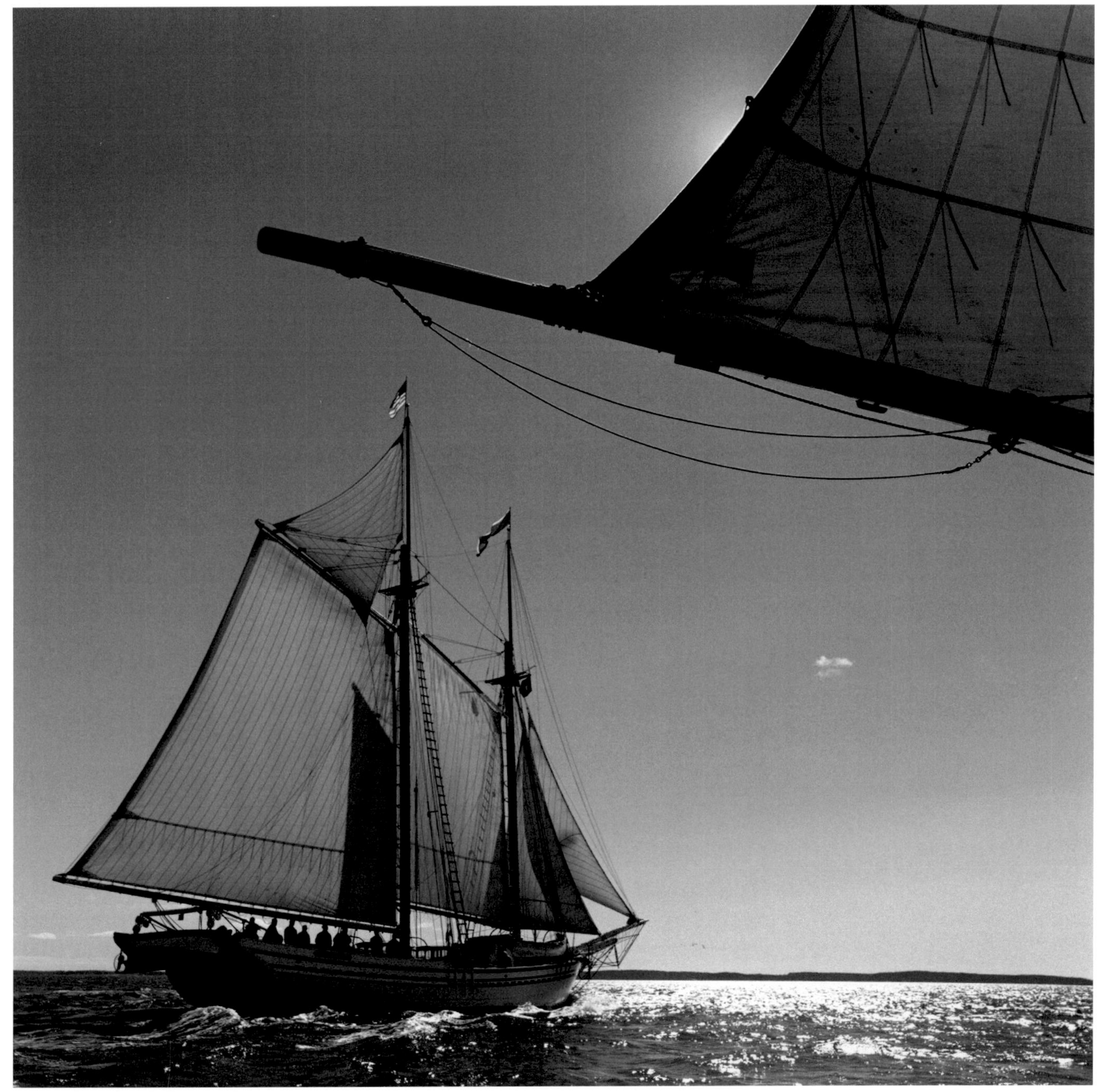

Heritage, 2010

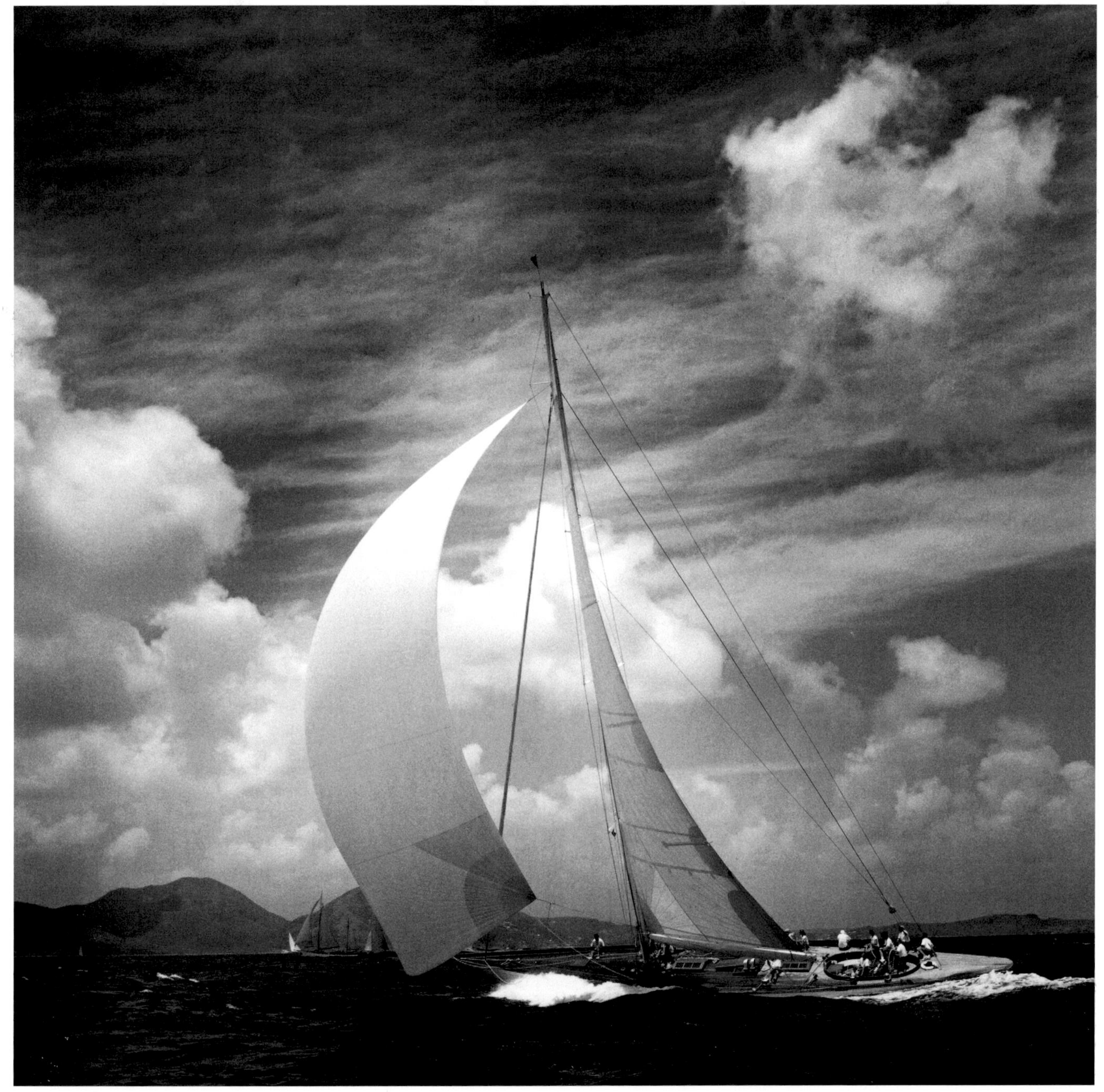

Savannah, 2001

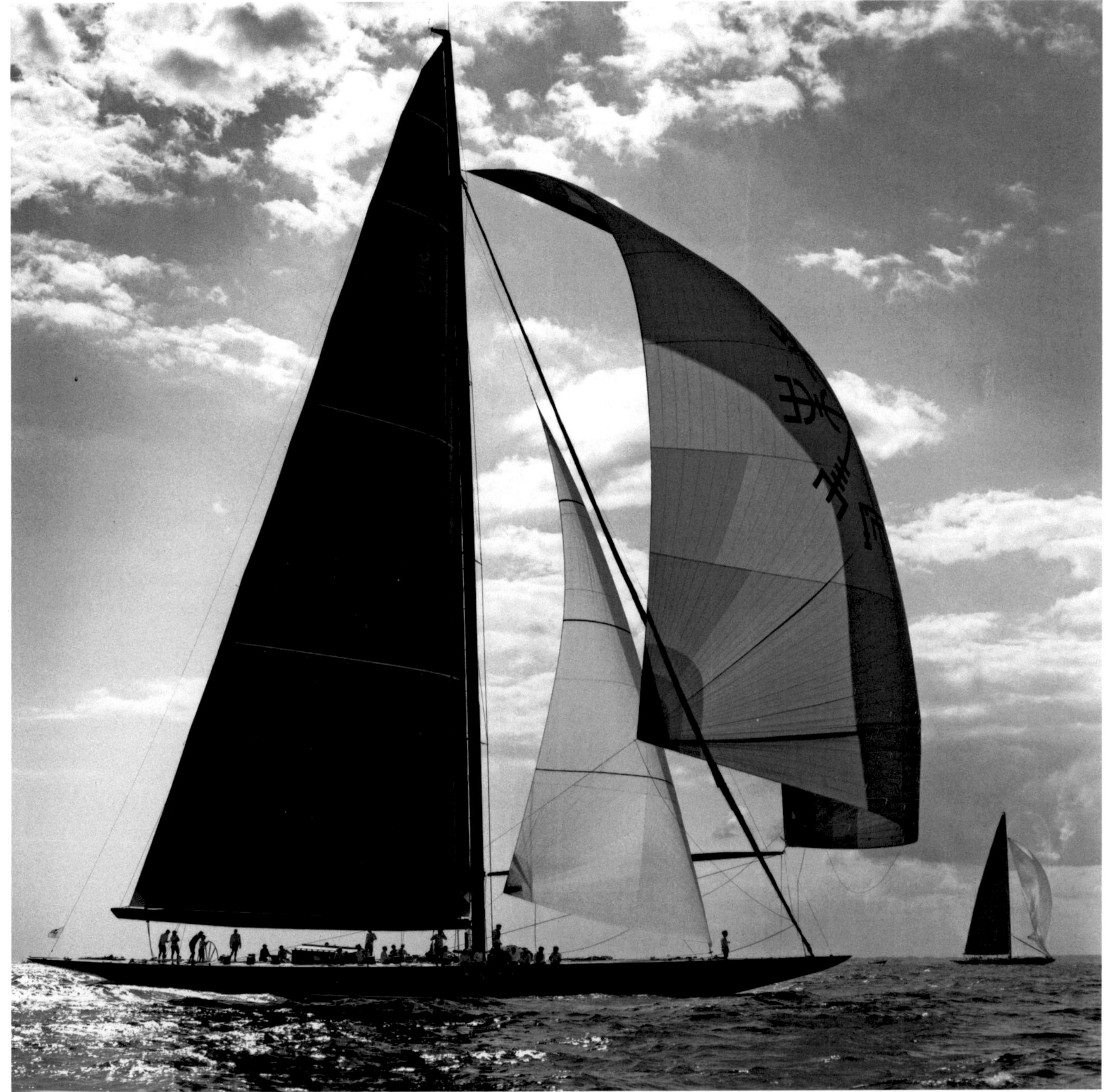

Svea, 2017

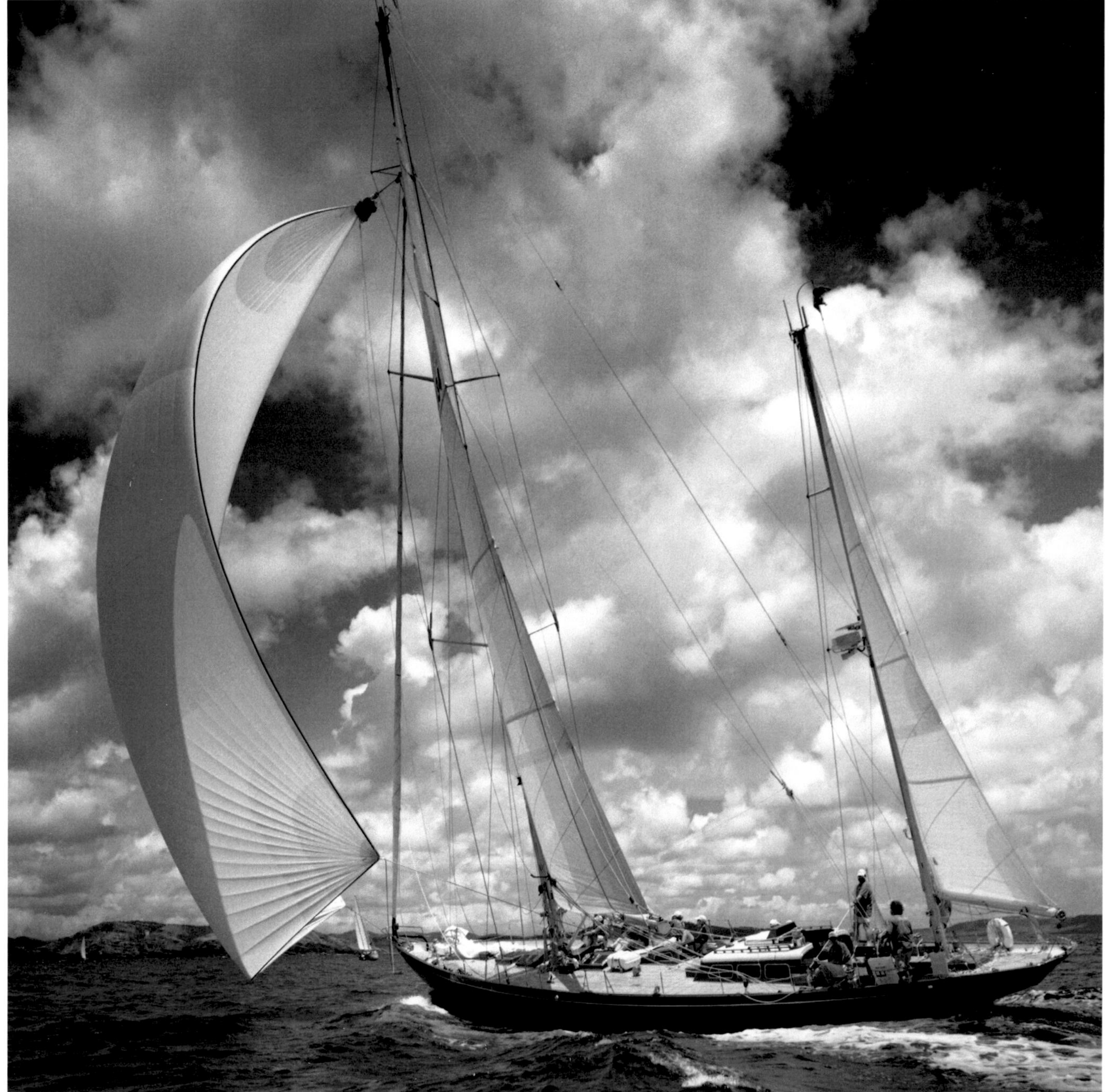

Bolero, 2011

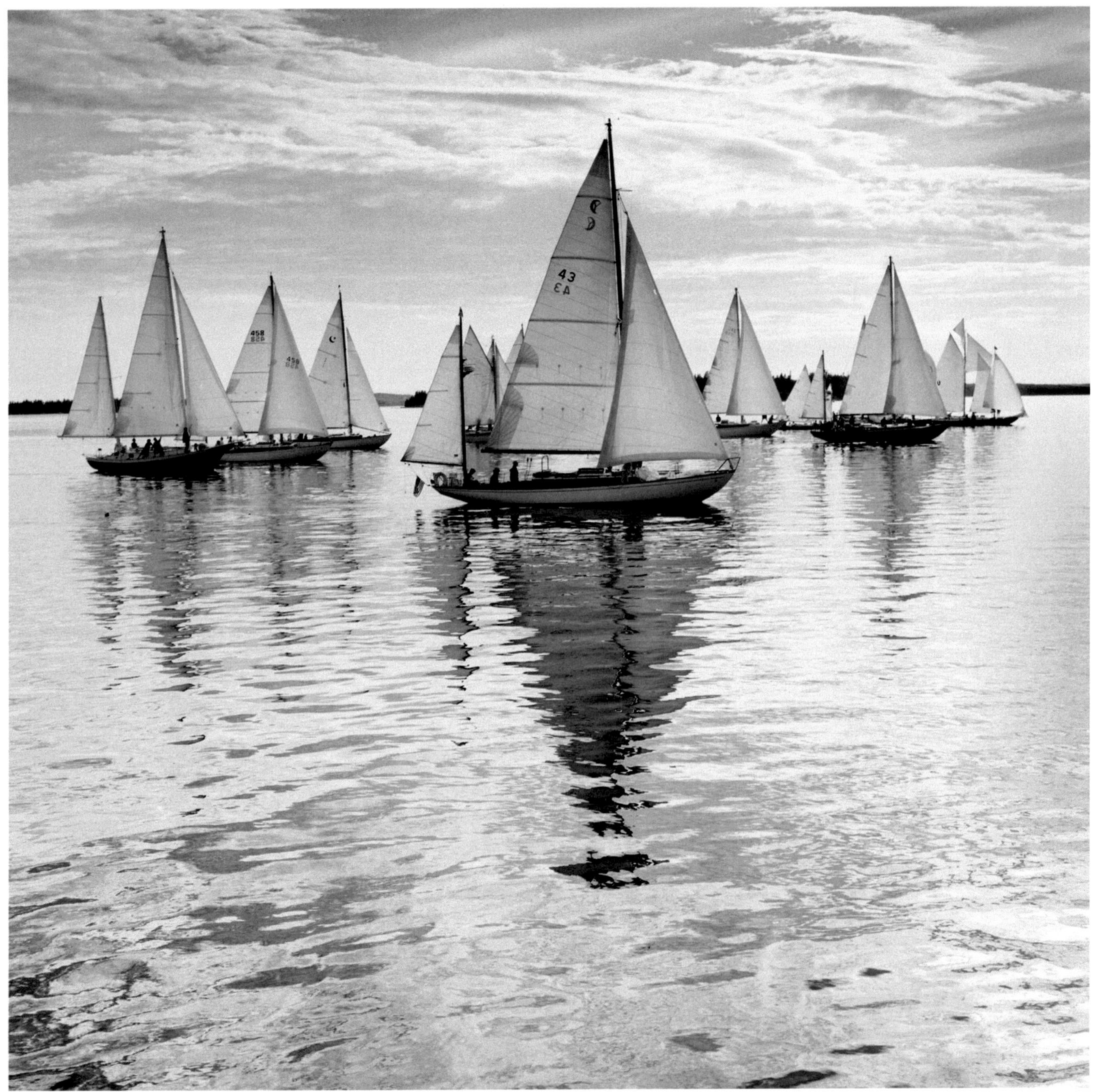

Classic Regatta, 2004

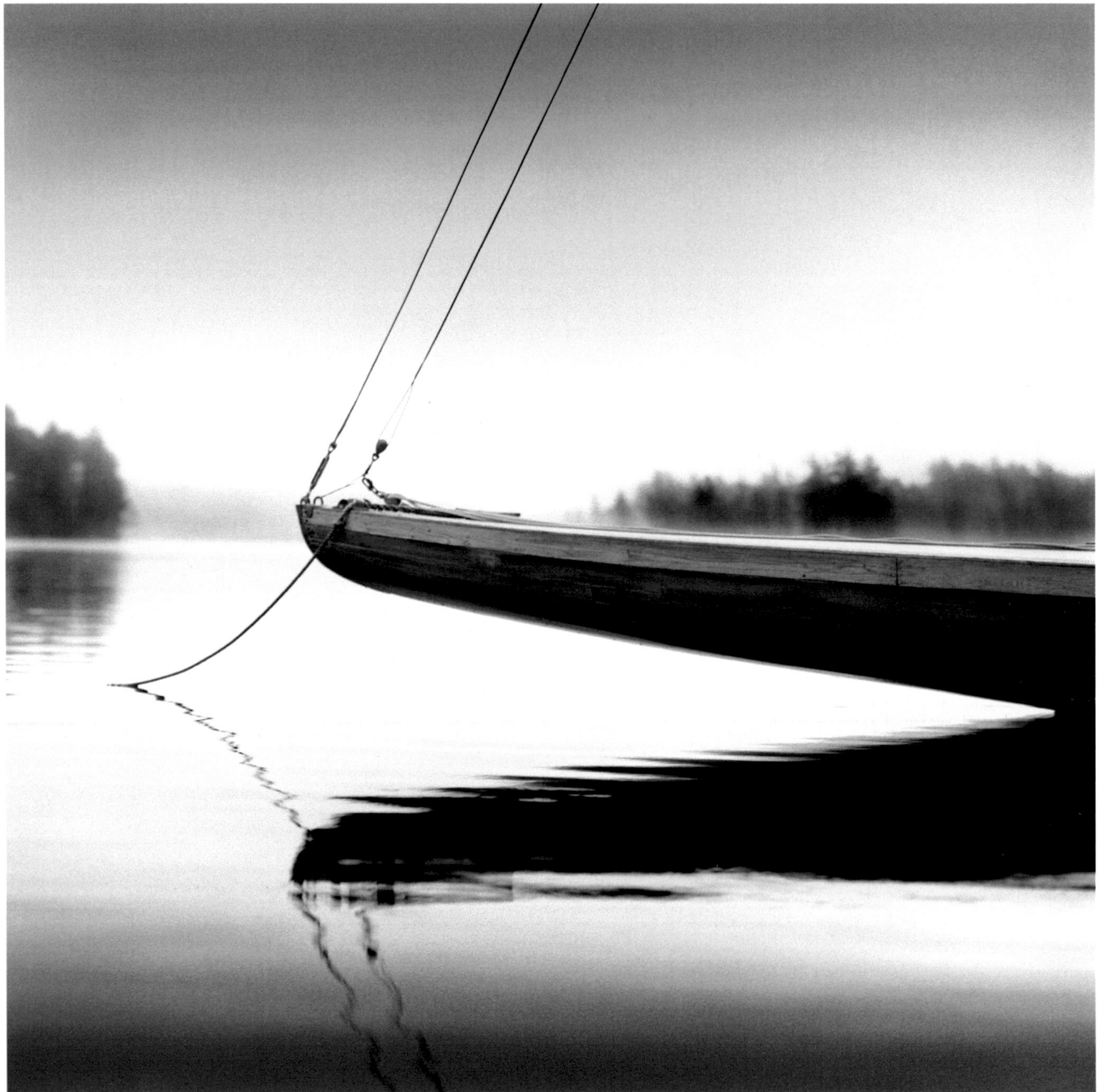

The Idem, 1996

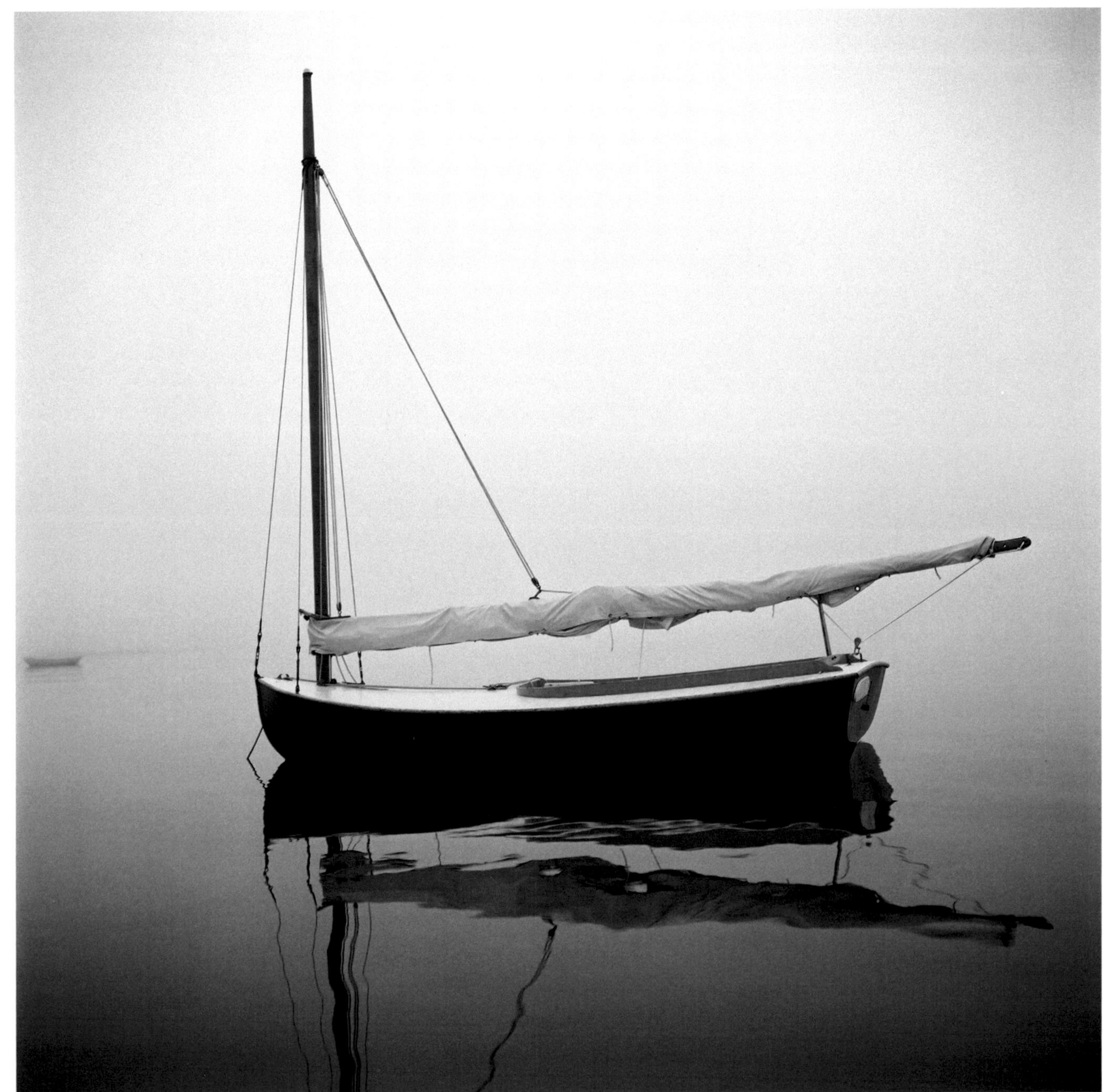

Whimsey, 2002

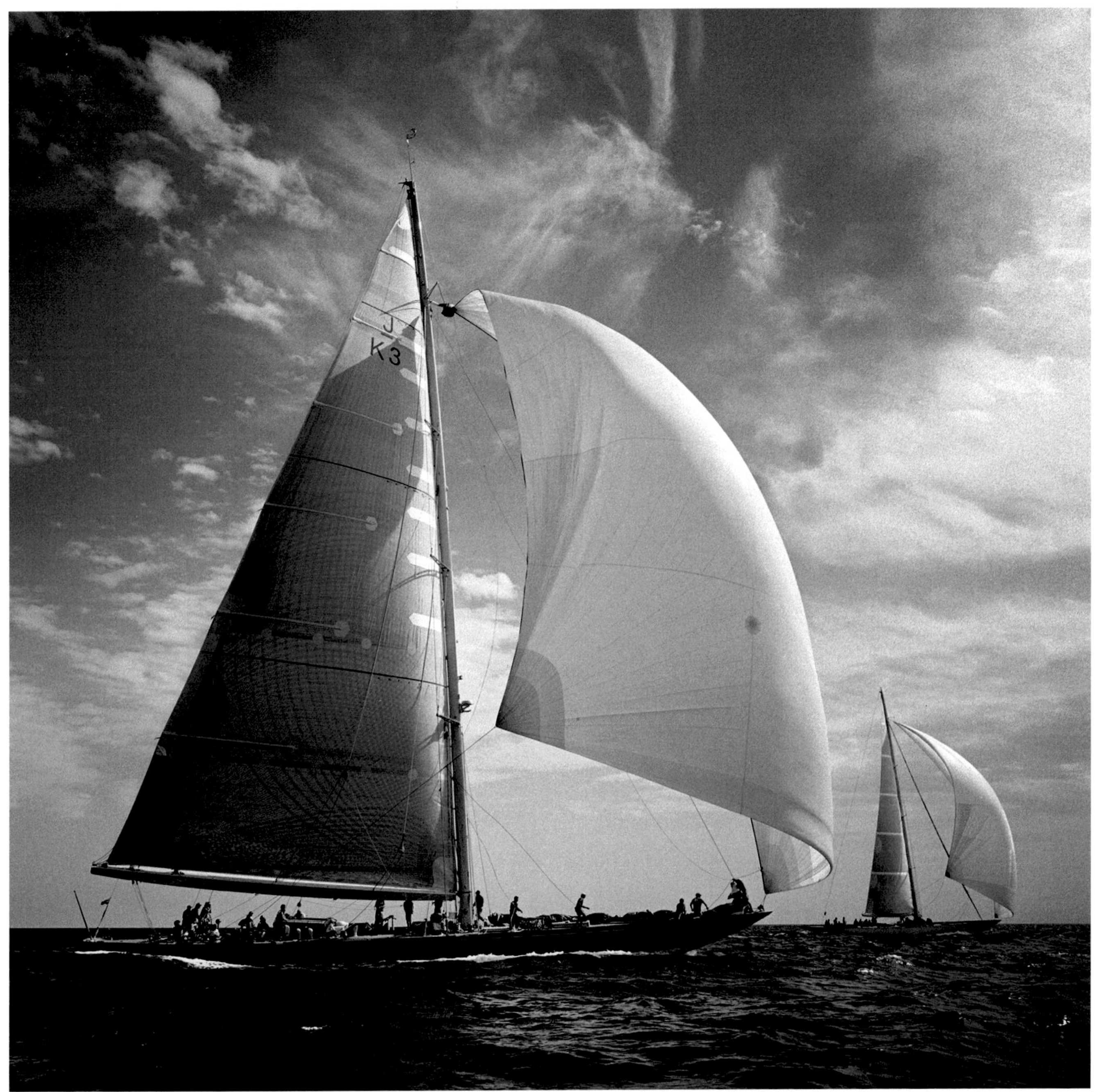

Shamrock V vs. Savannah, 2007

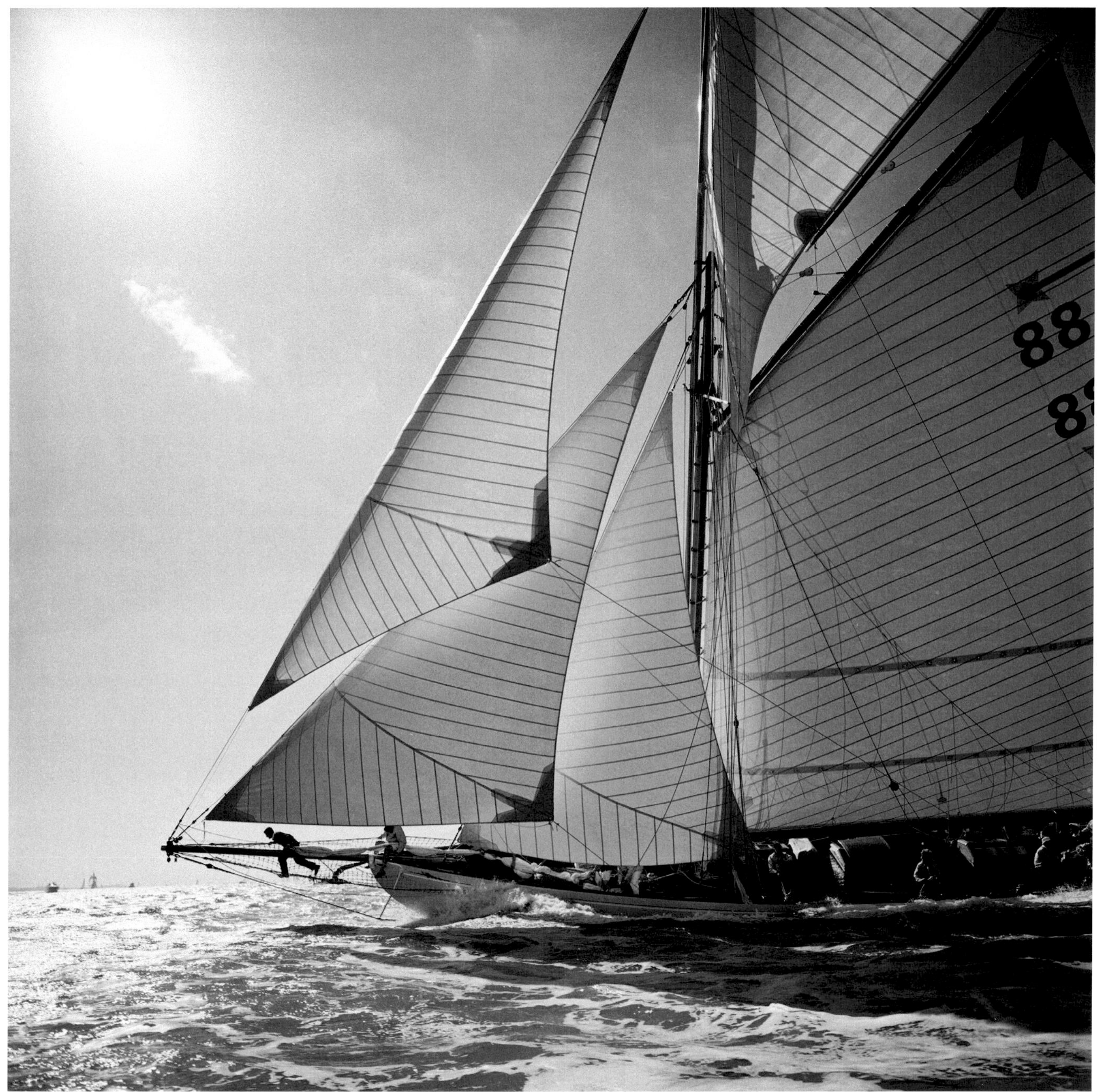

Moonbeam of Fife, 2001

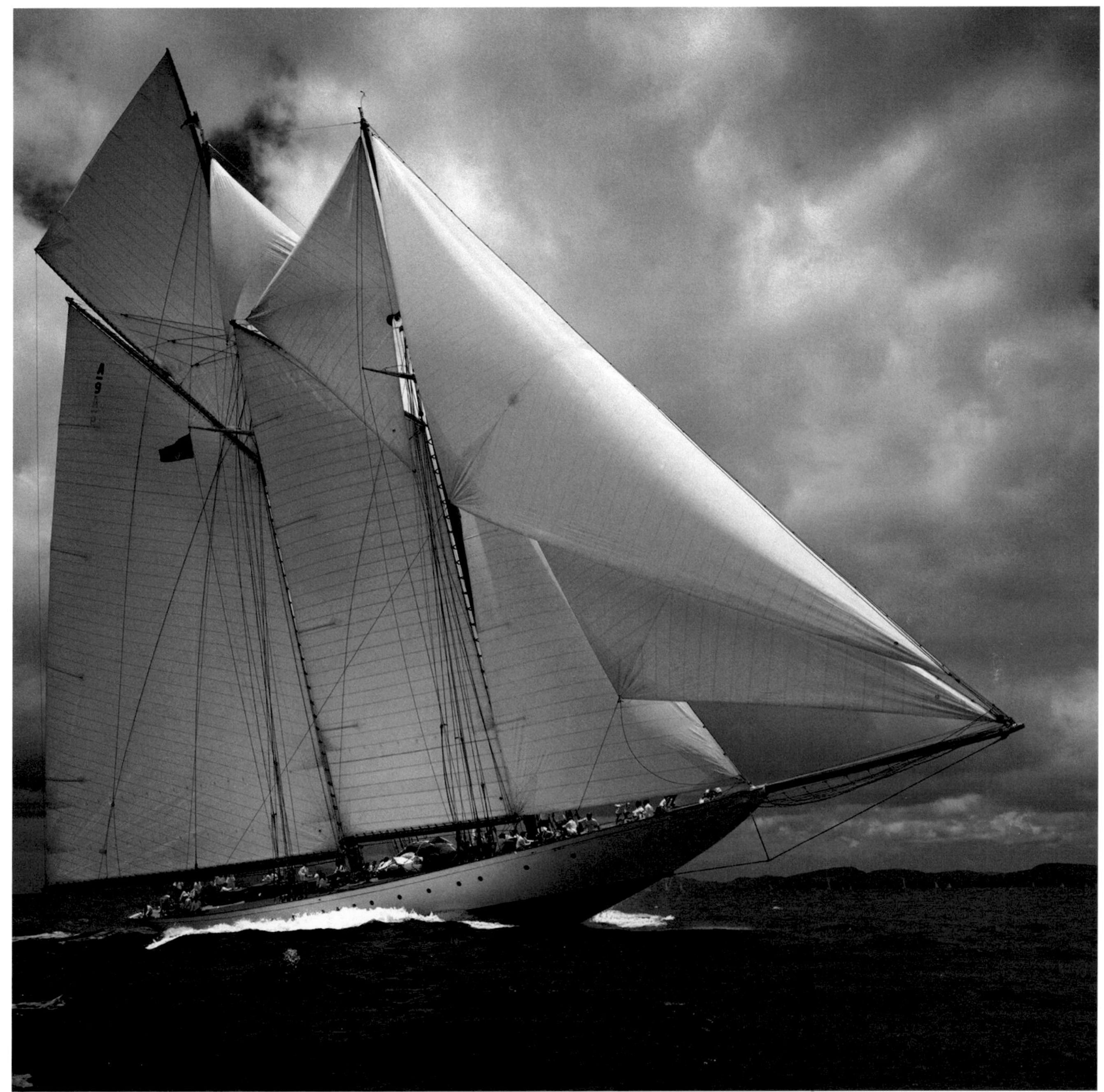

Elena, 2011

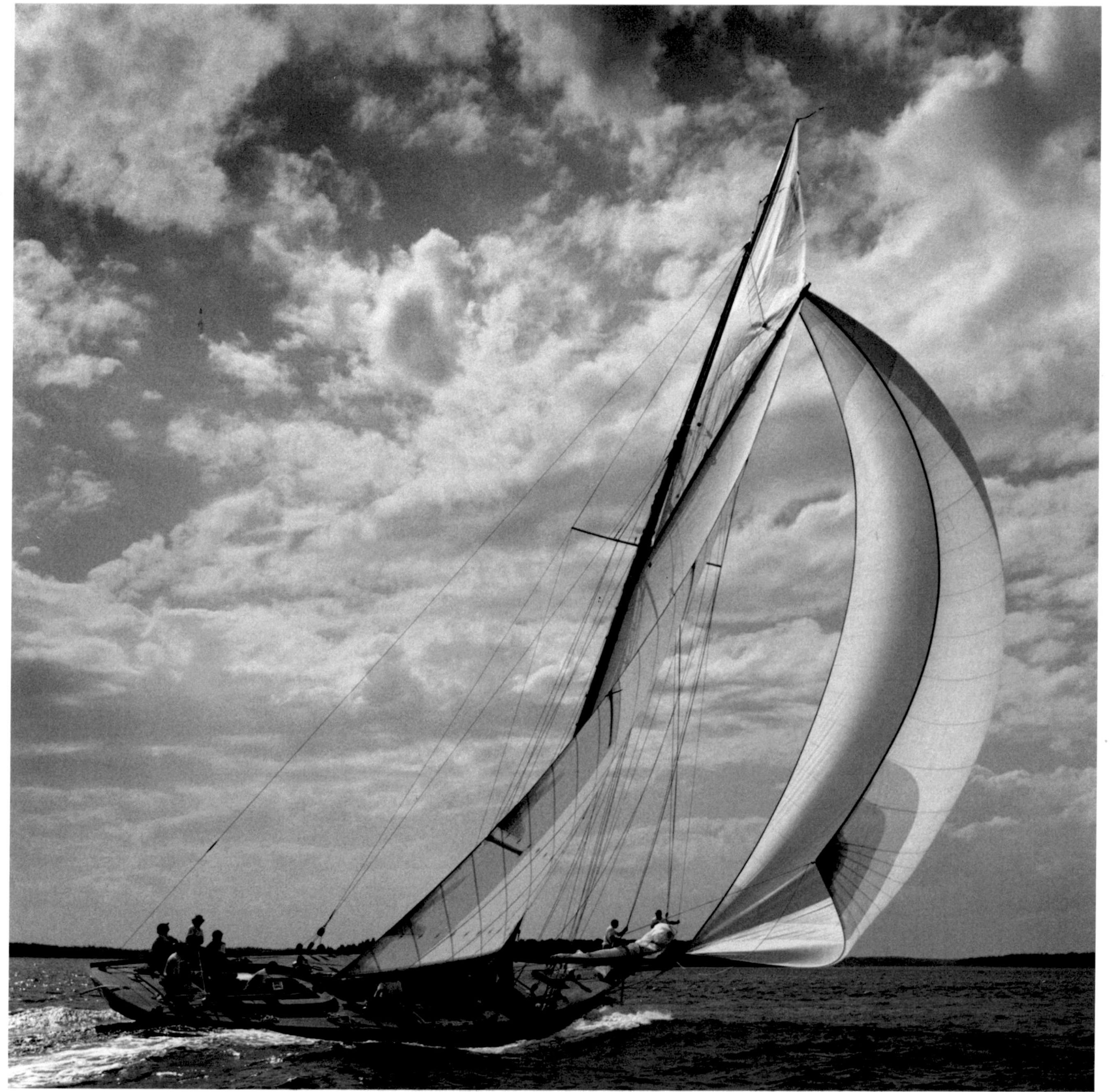

Spartan, 2010

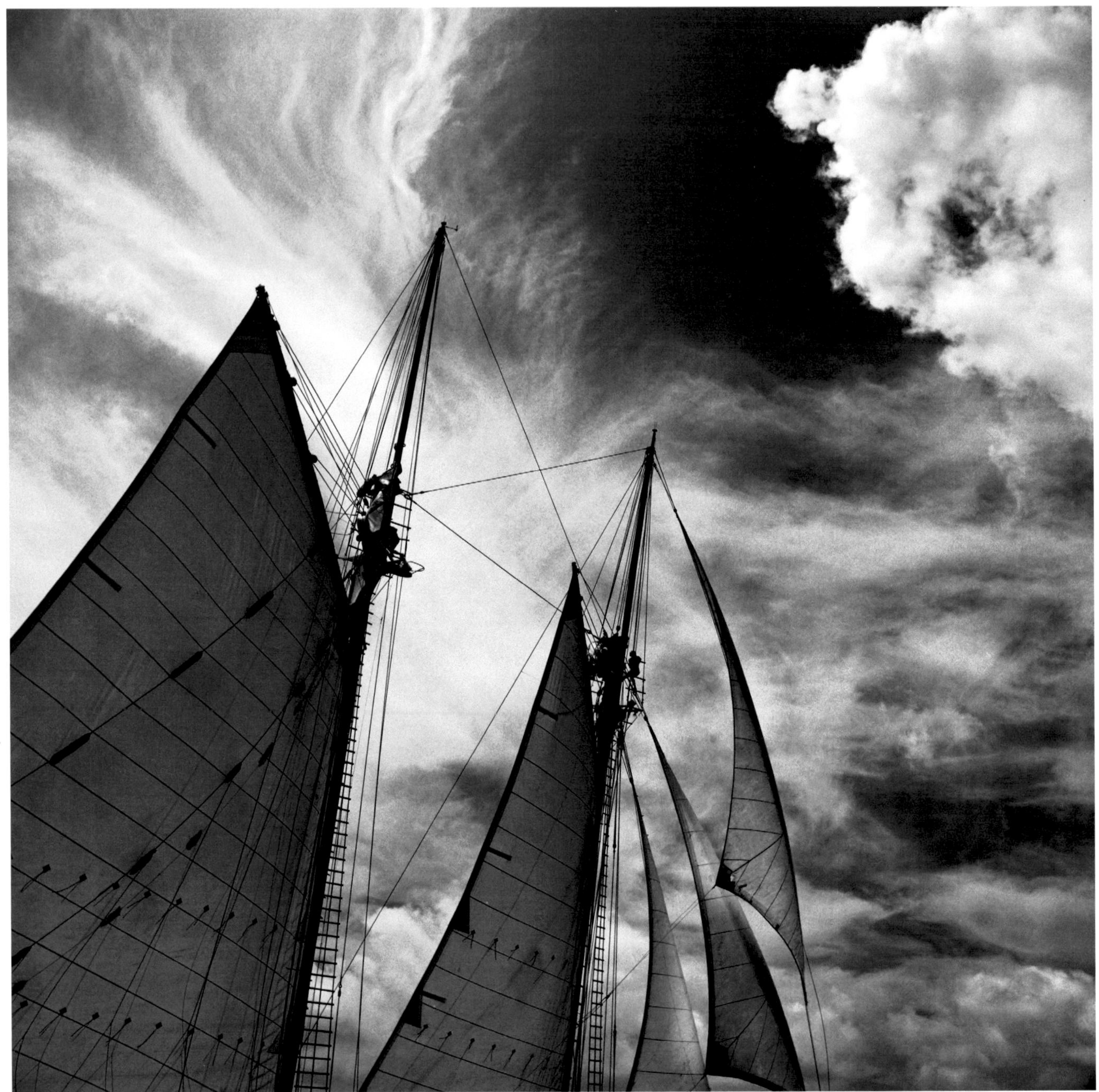

Highlander Sea, 2000

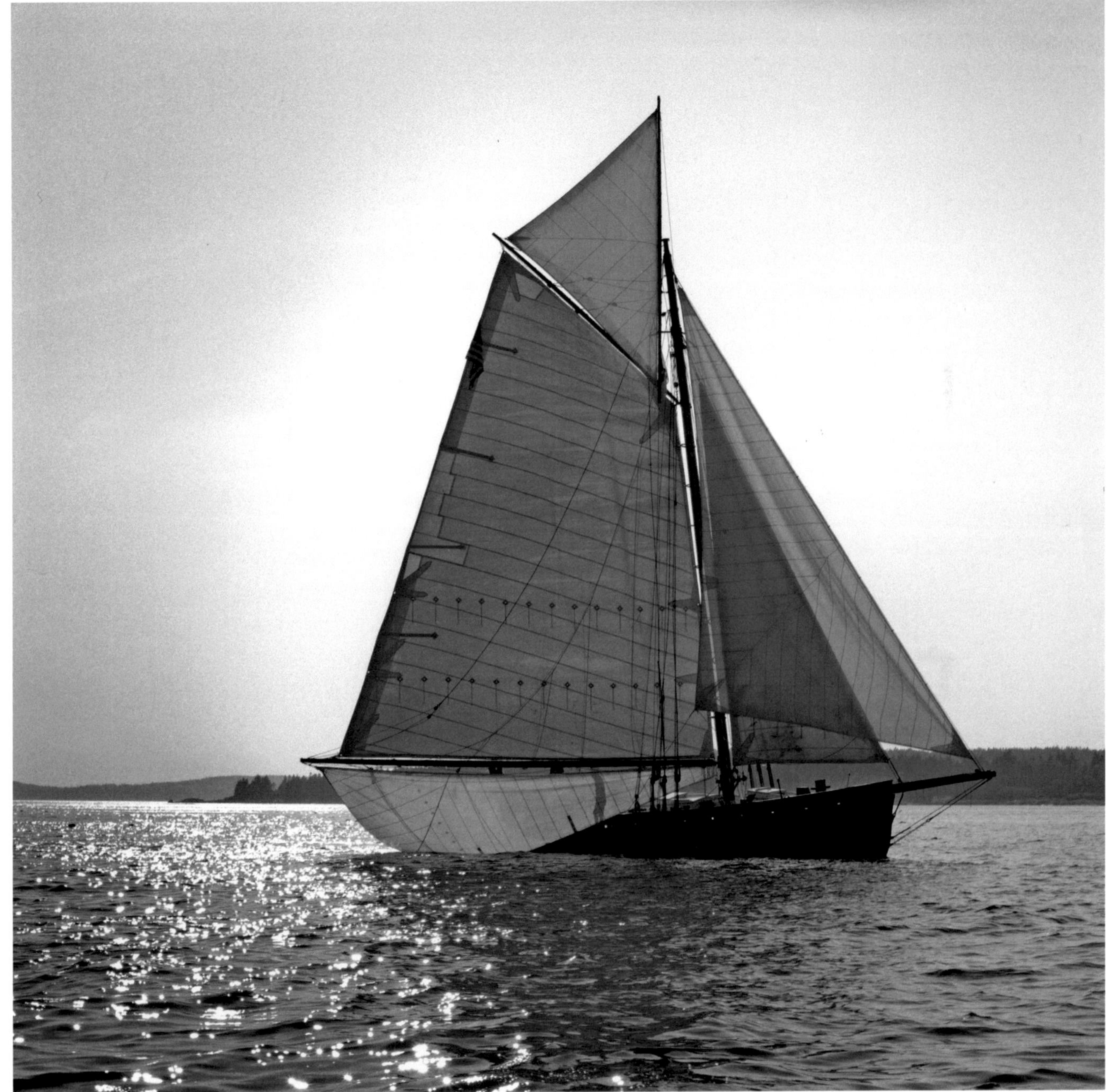

Vela, 2014

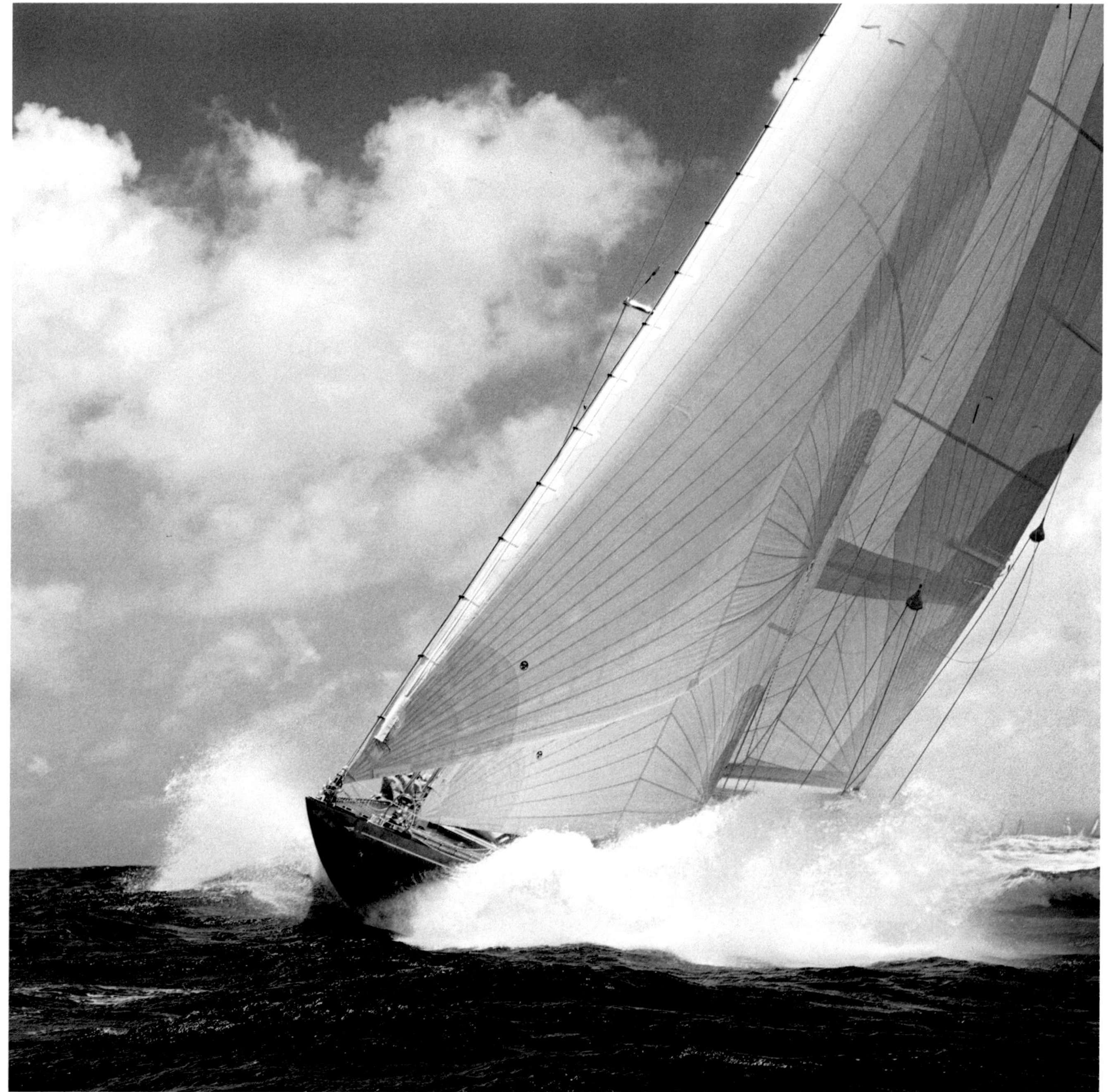

Velsheda, 2001

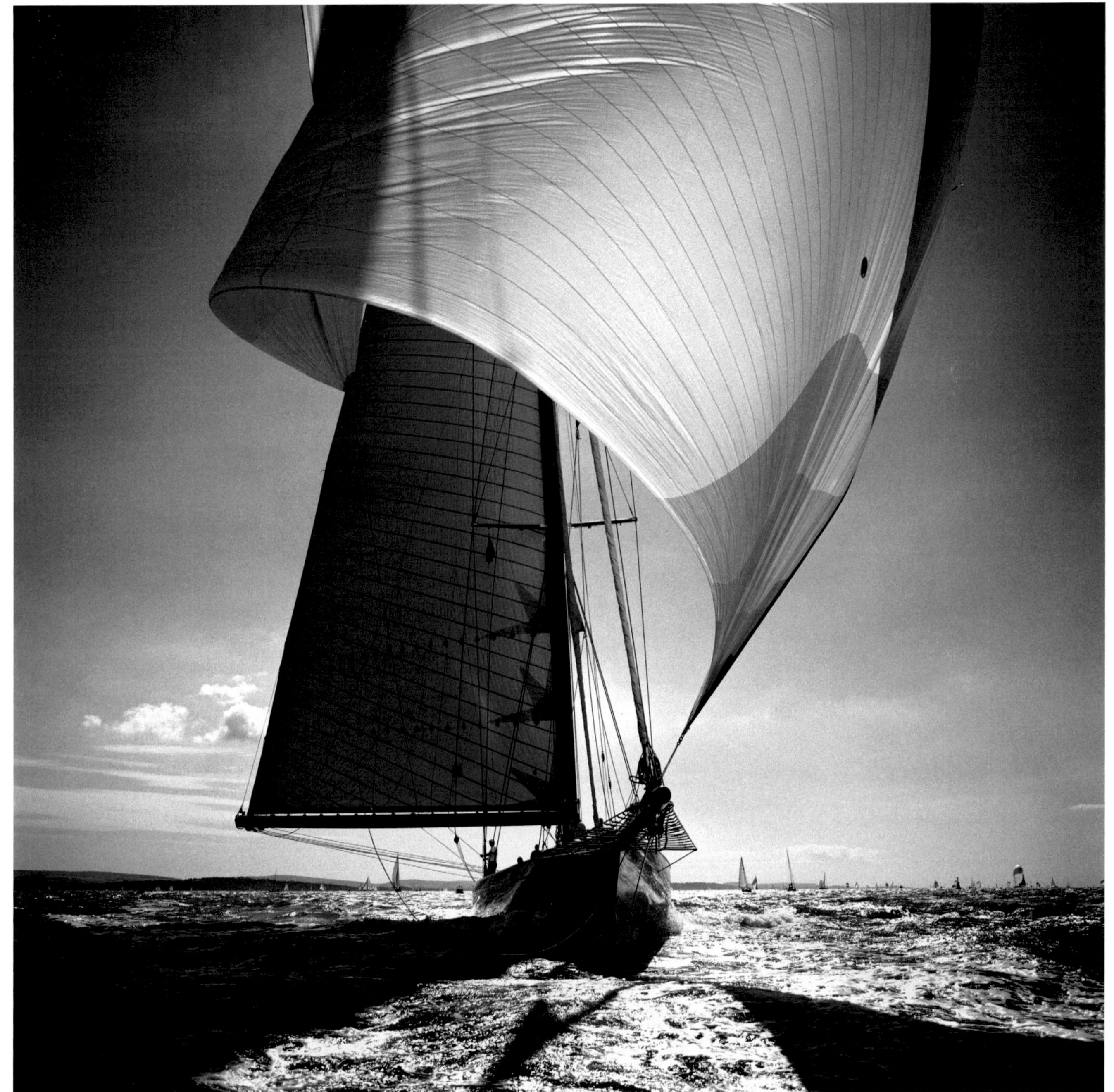

Cambria, 2001

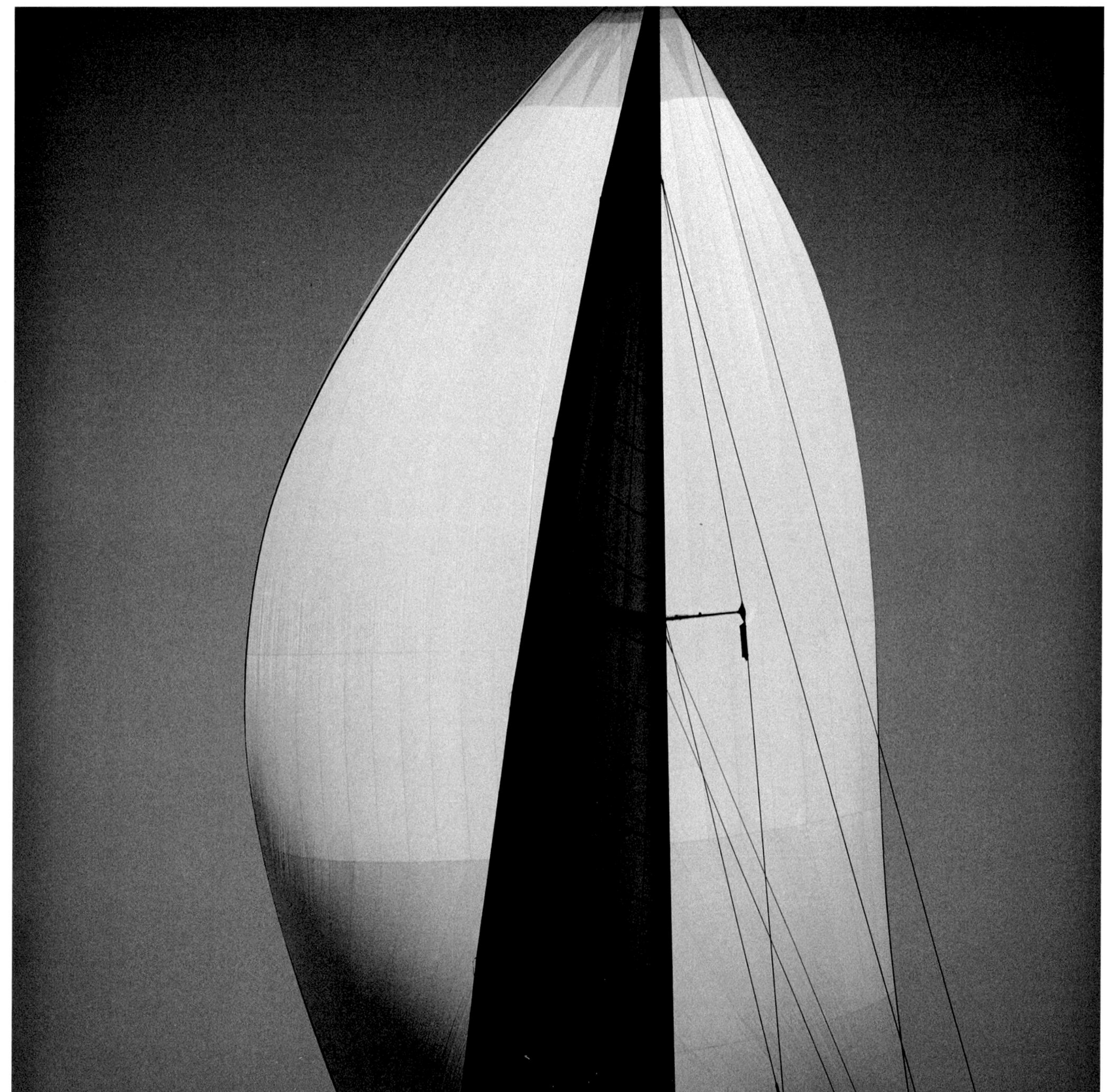

Wild Horses, 1998

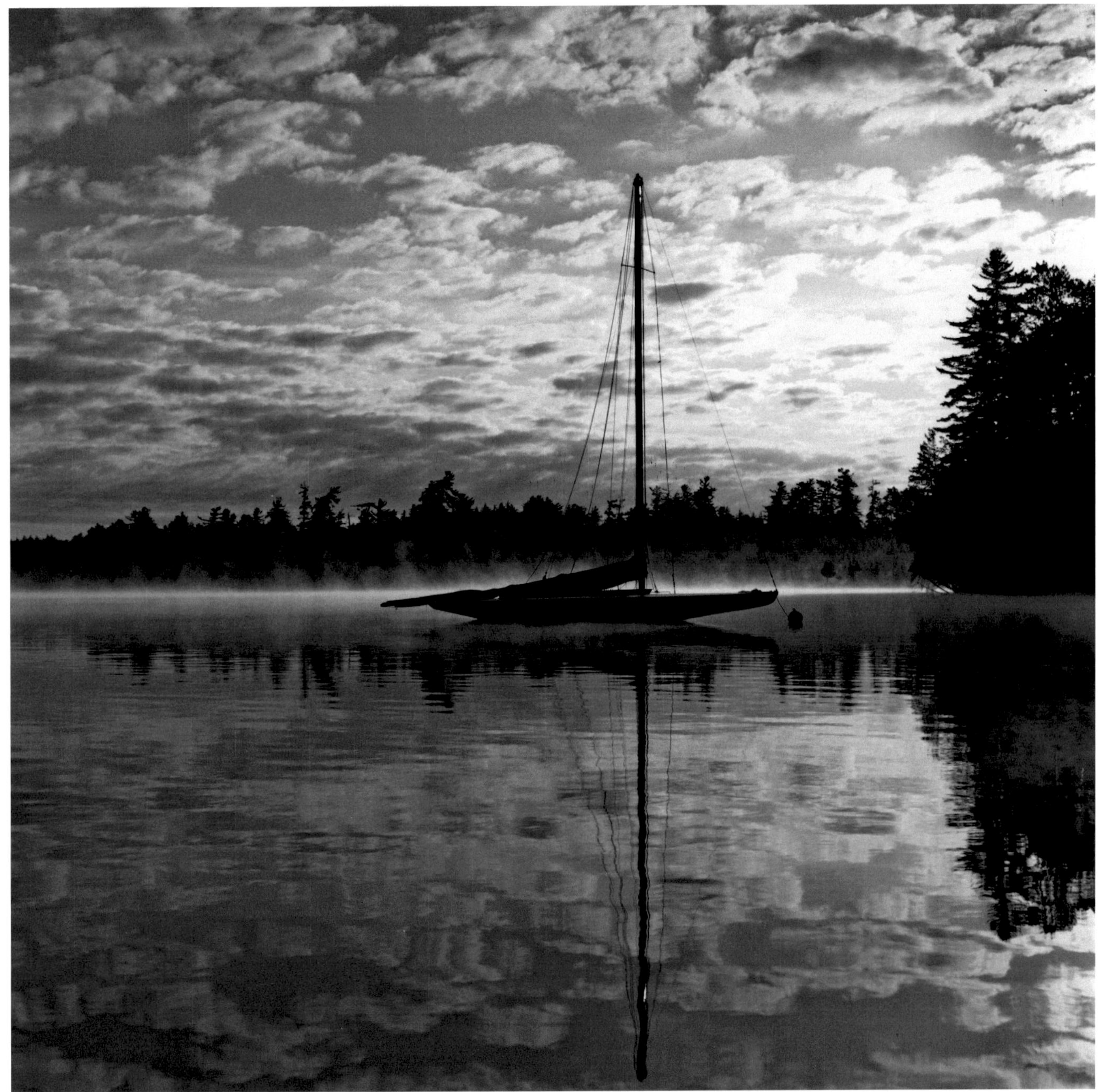

The Idem, 2012

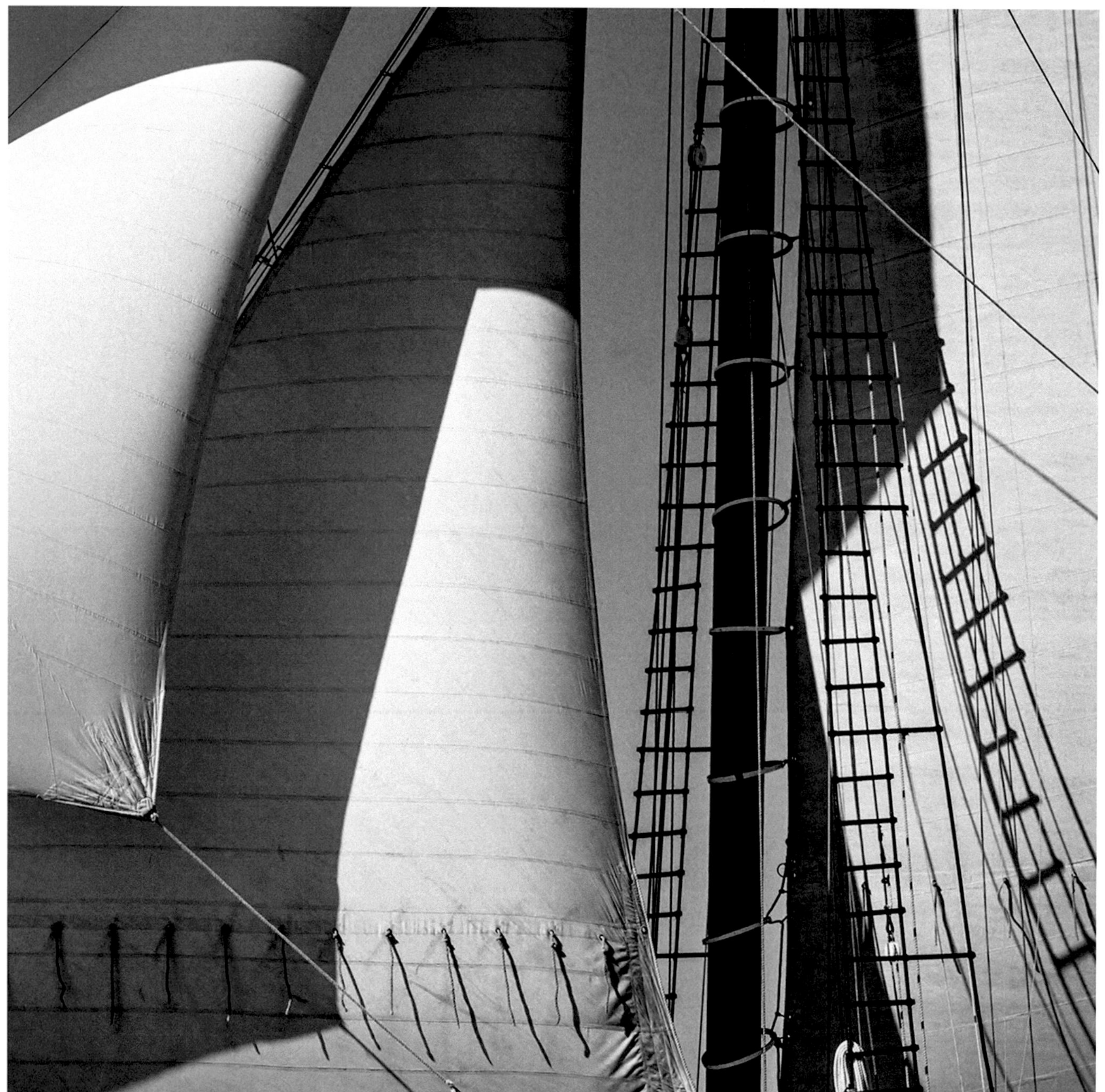

Mary Day, 1998

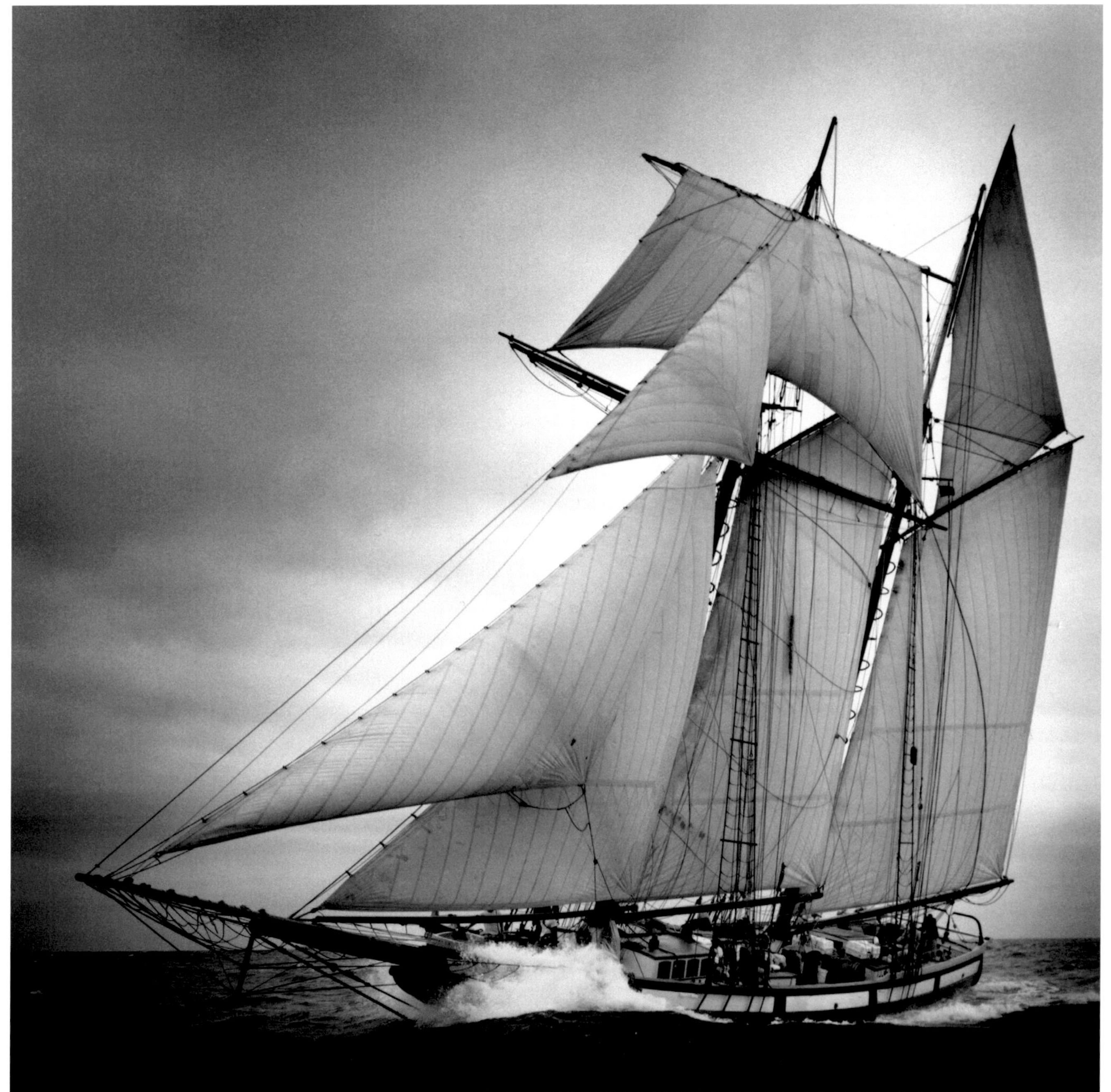

The Lynx, 2018

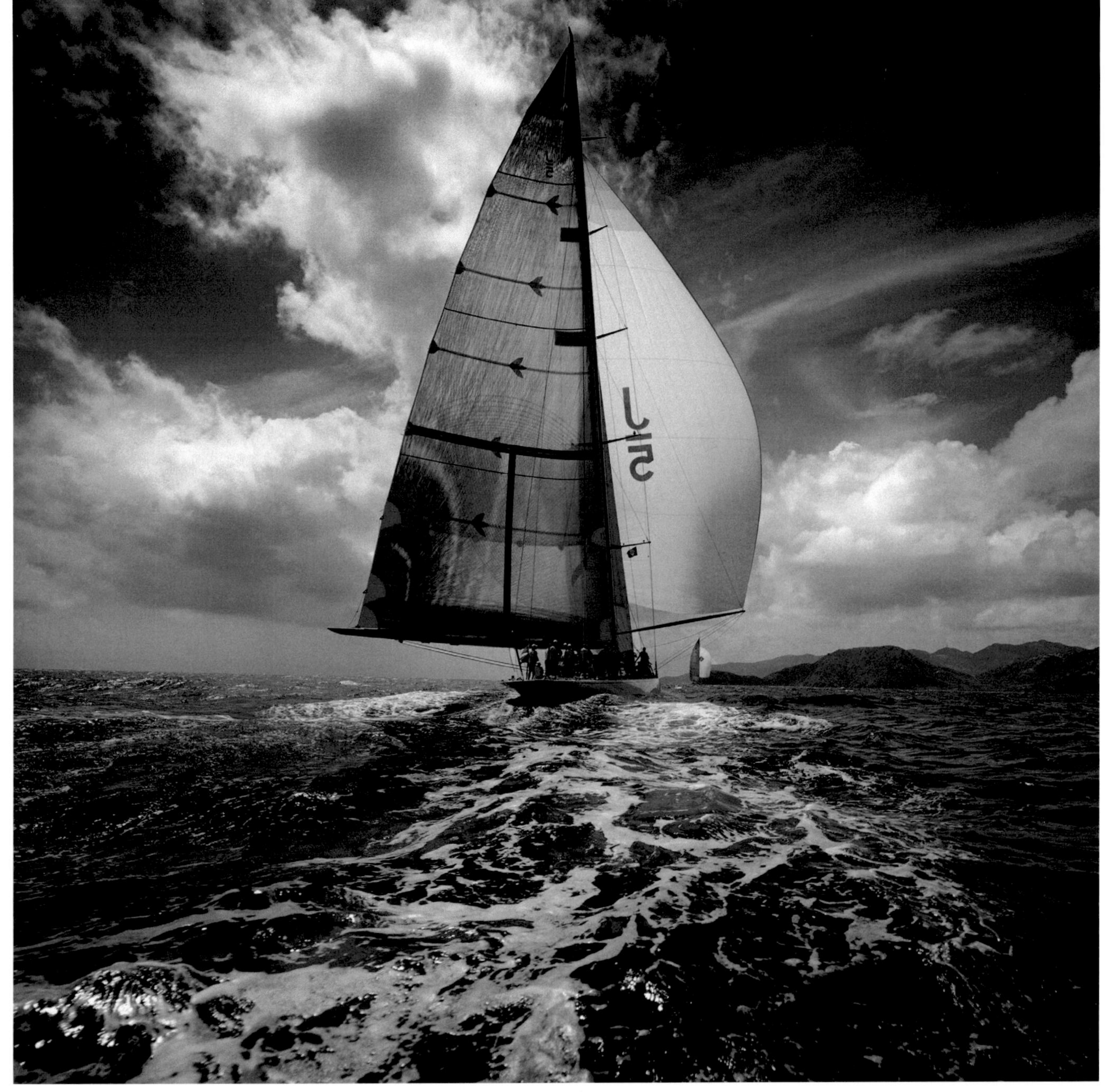

Ranger, 2004

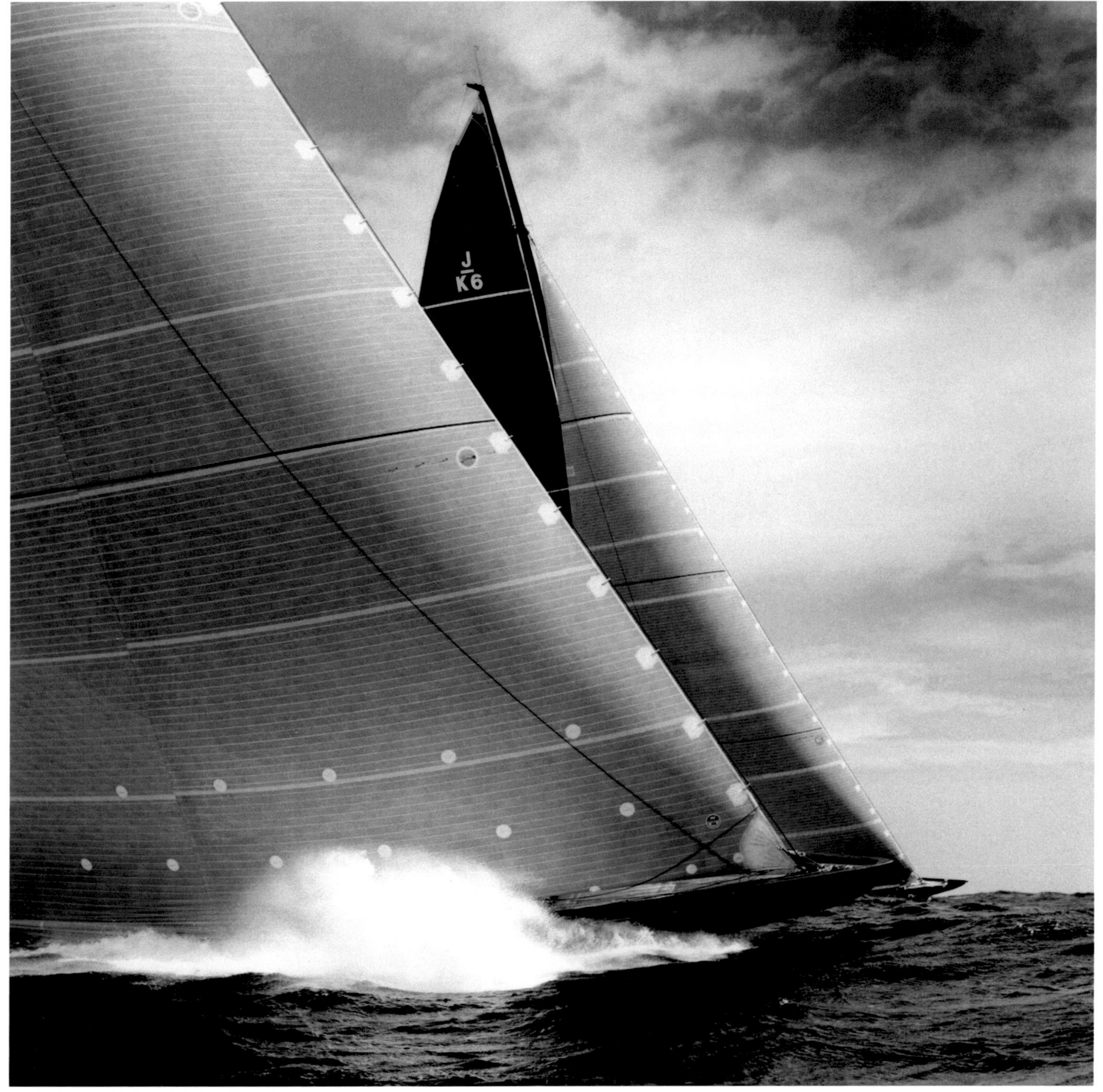

Lionheart vs. Hanuman, 2017

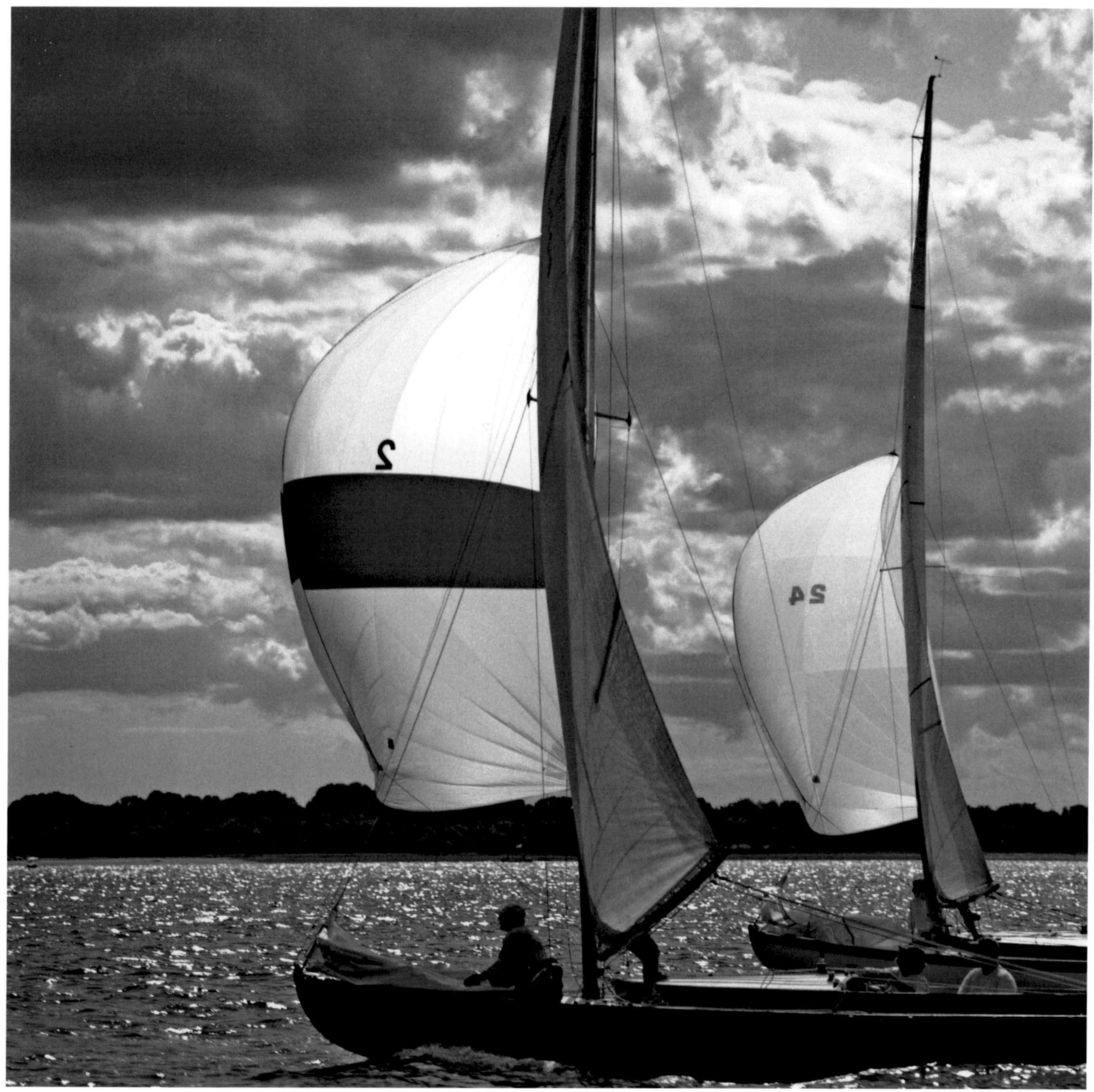

S Boats Racing, 2017

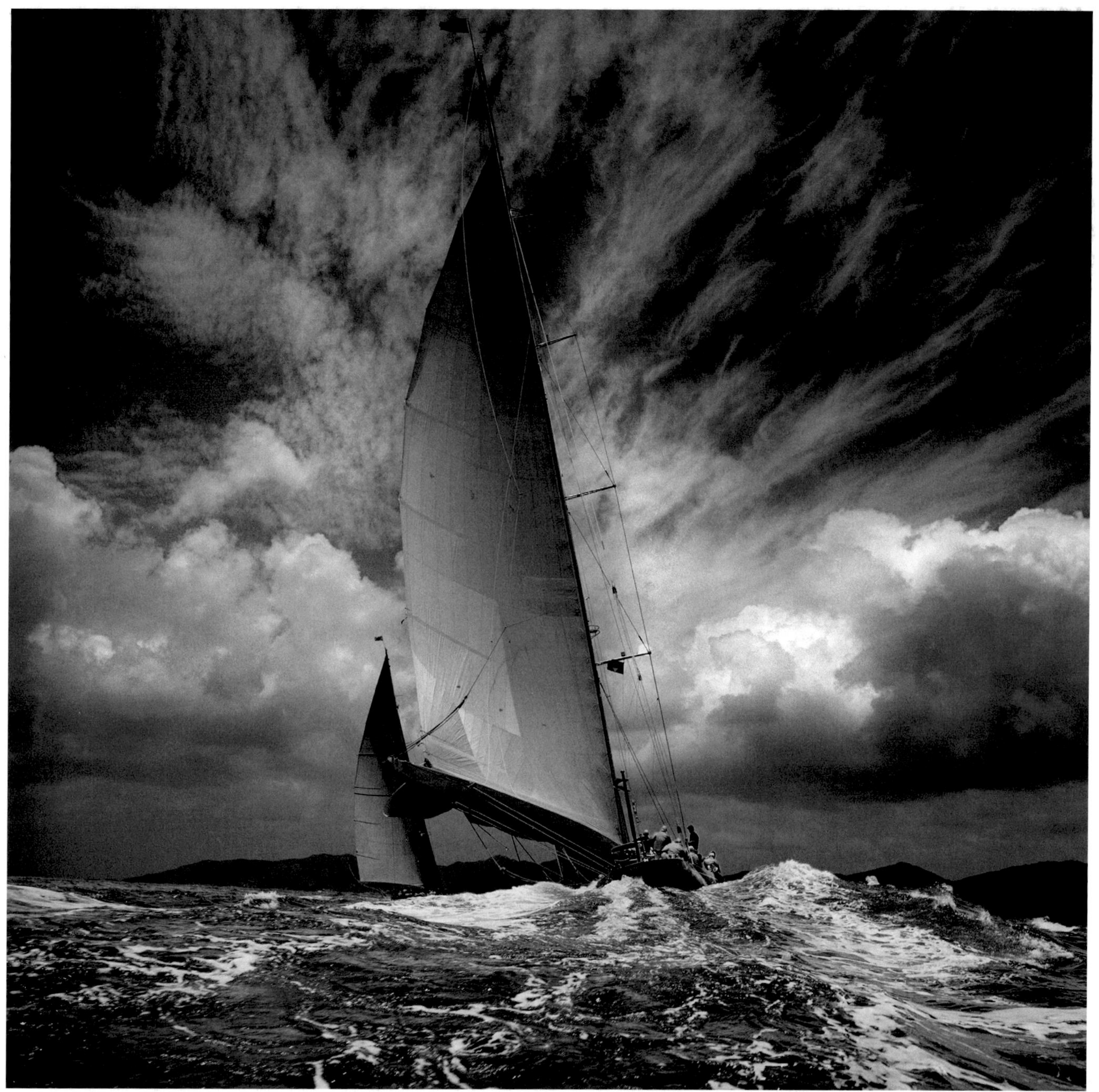

Velsehda vs. Endeavour, 2001

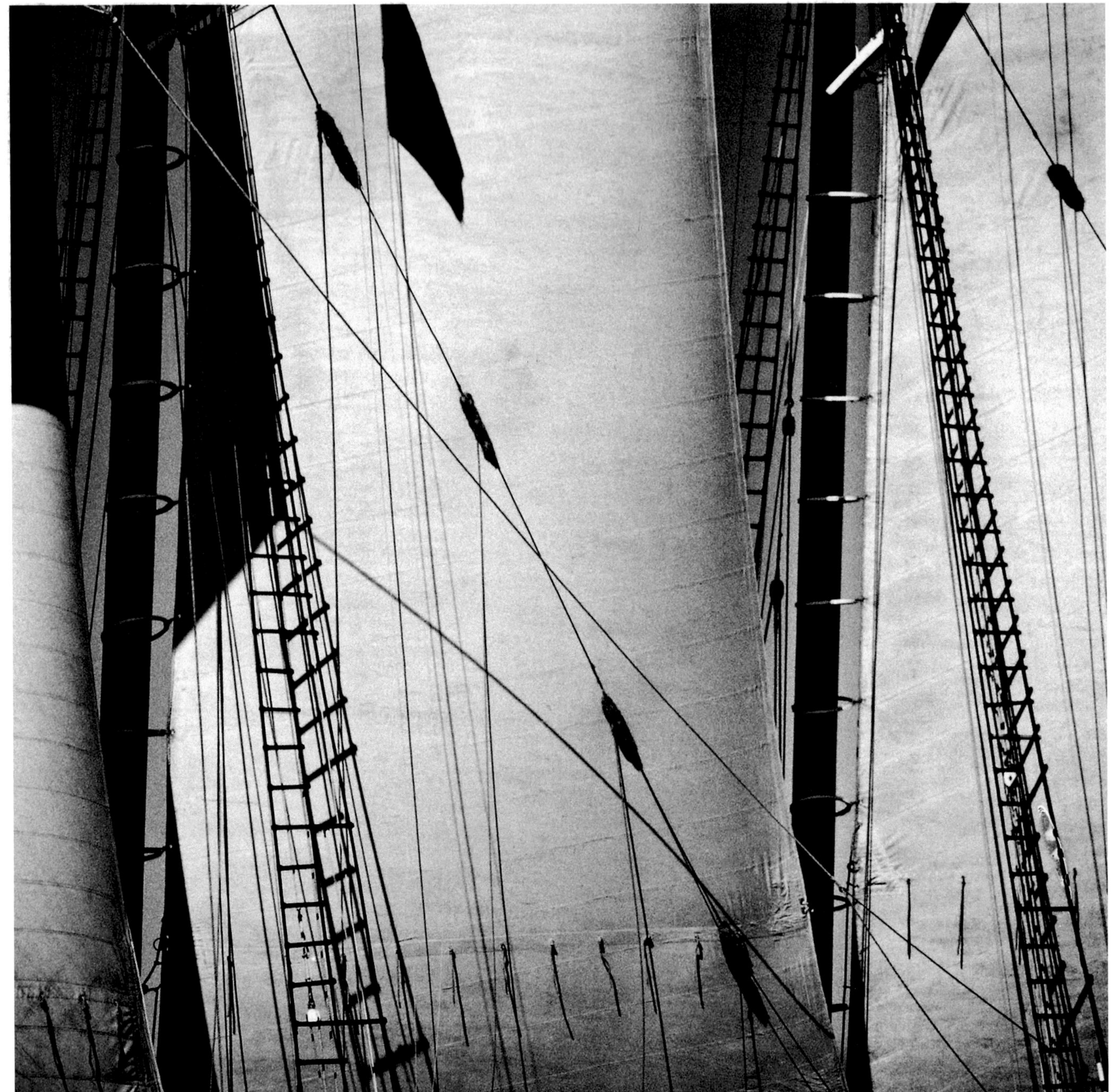

Mary Day, 1998

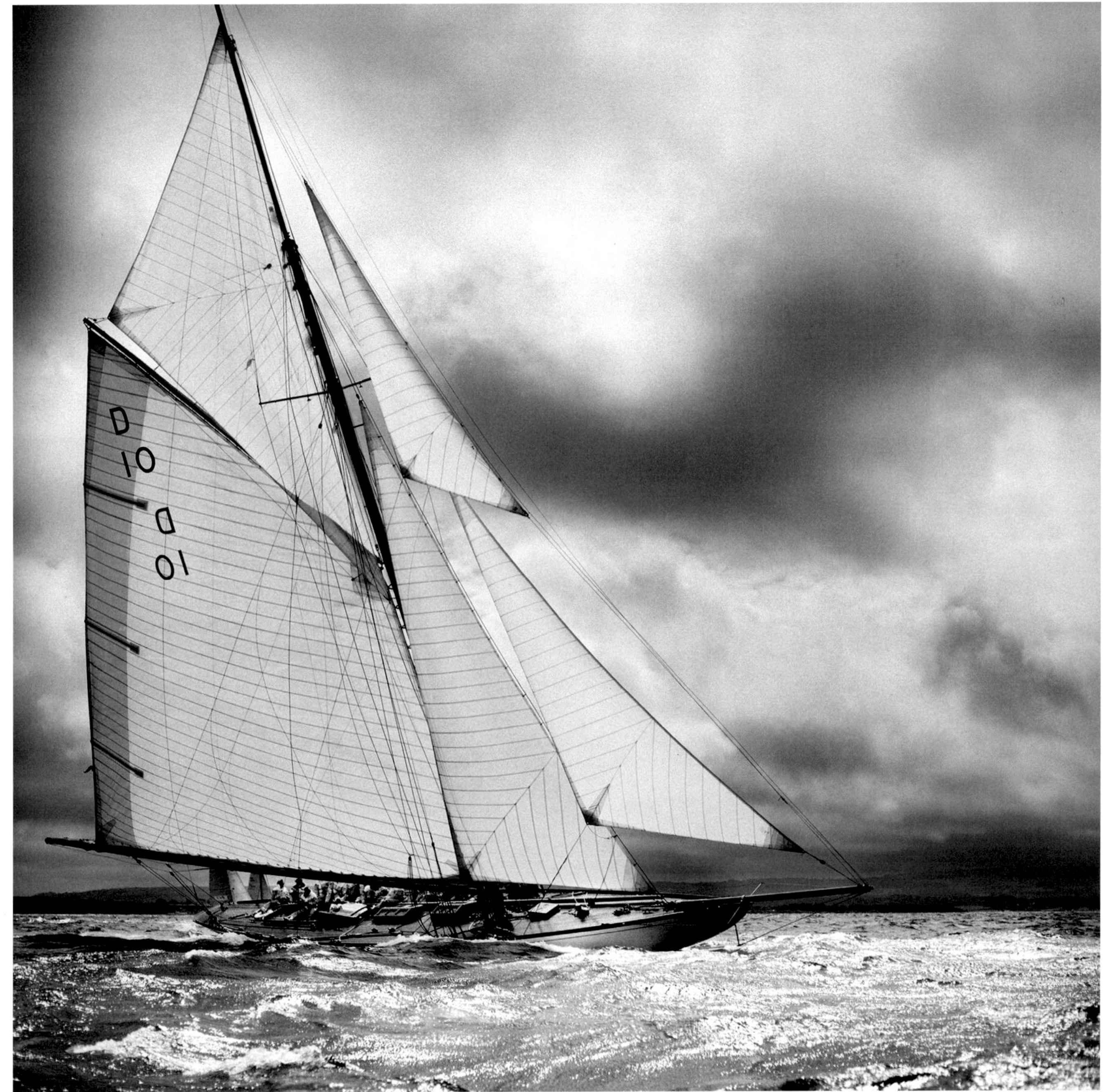

The Lady Anne, 2001

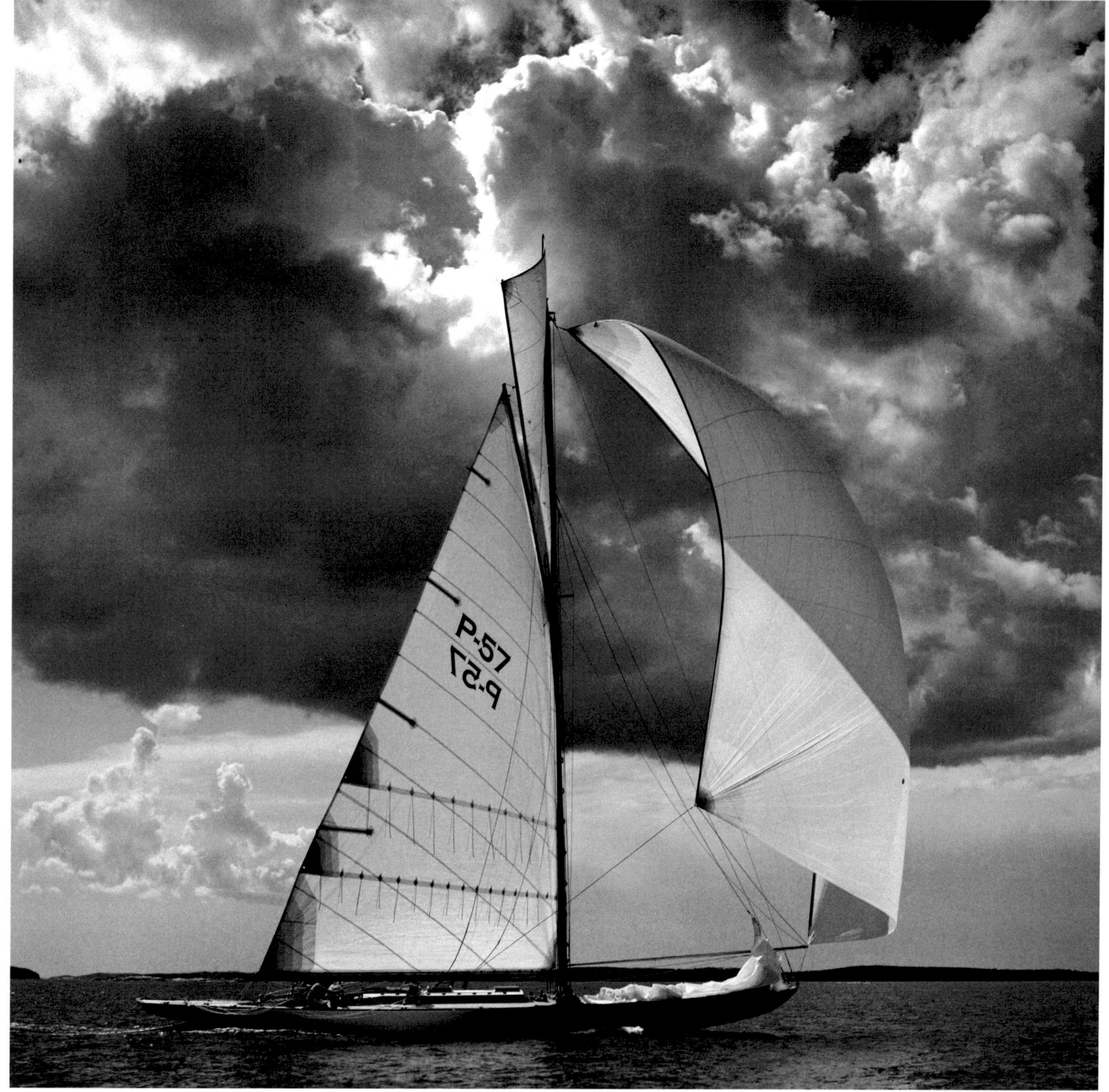

Joyant, 2004

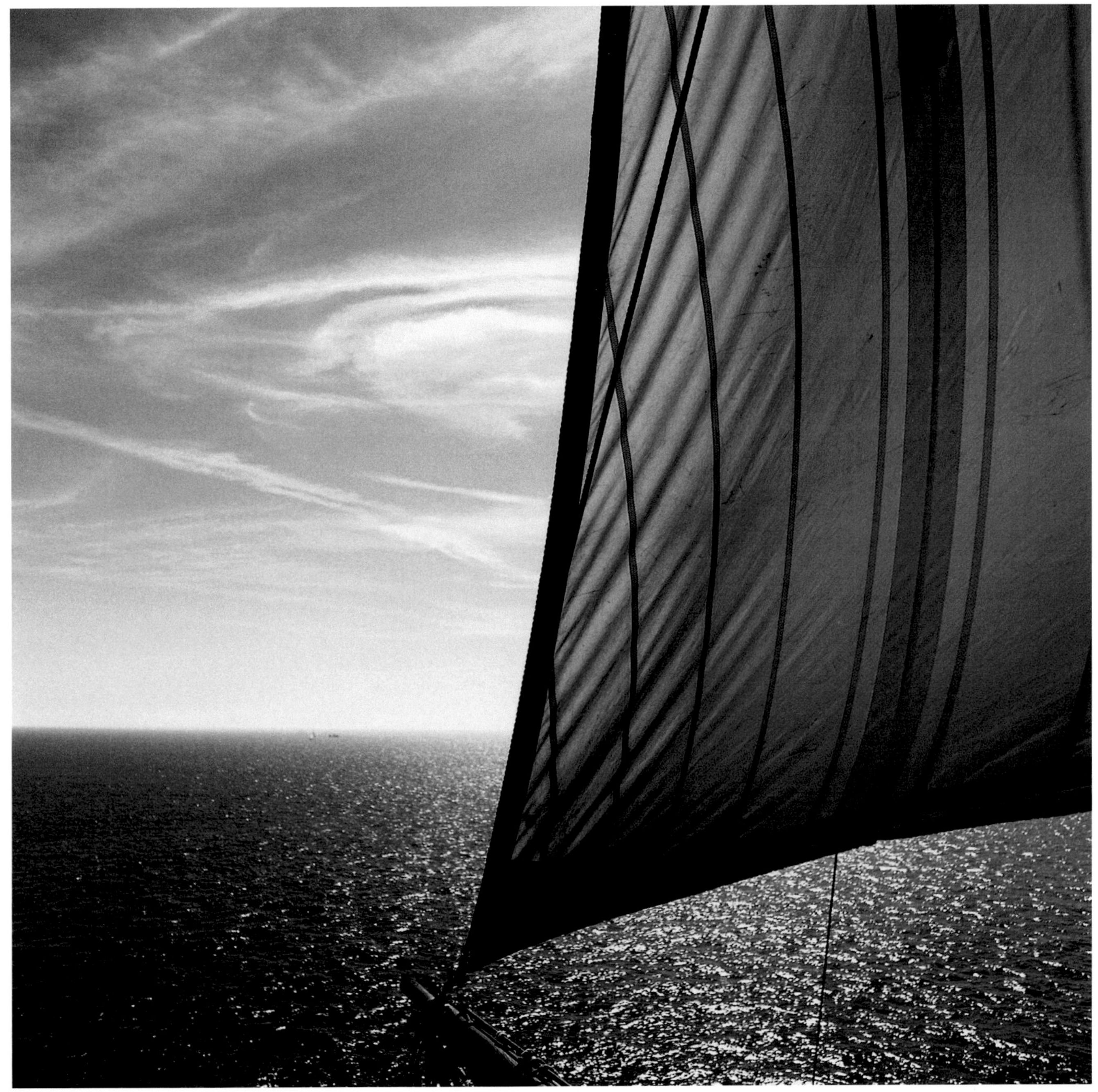

HMS Rose, 2000

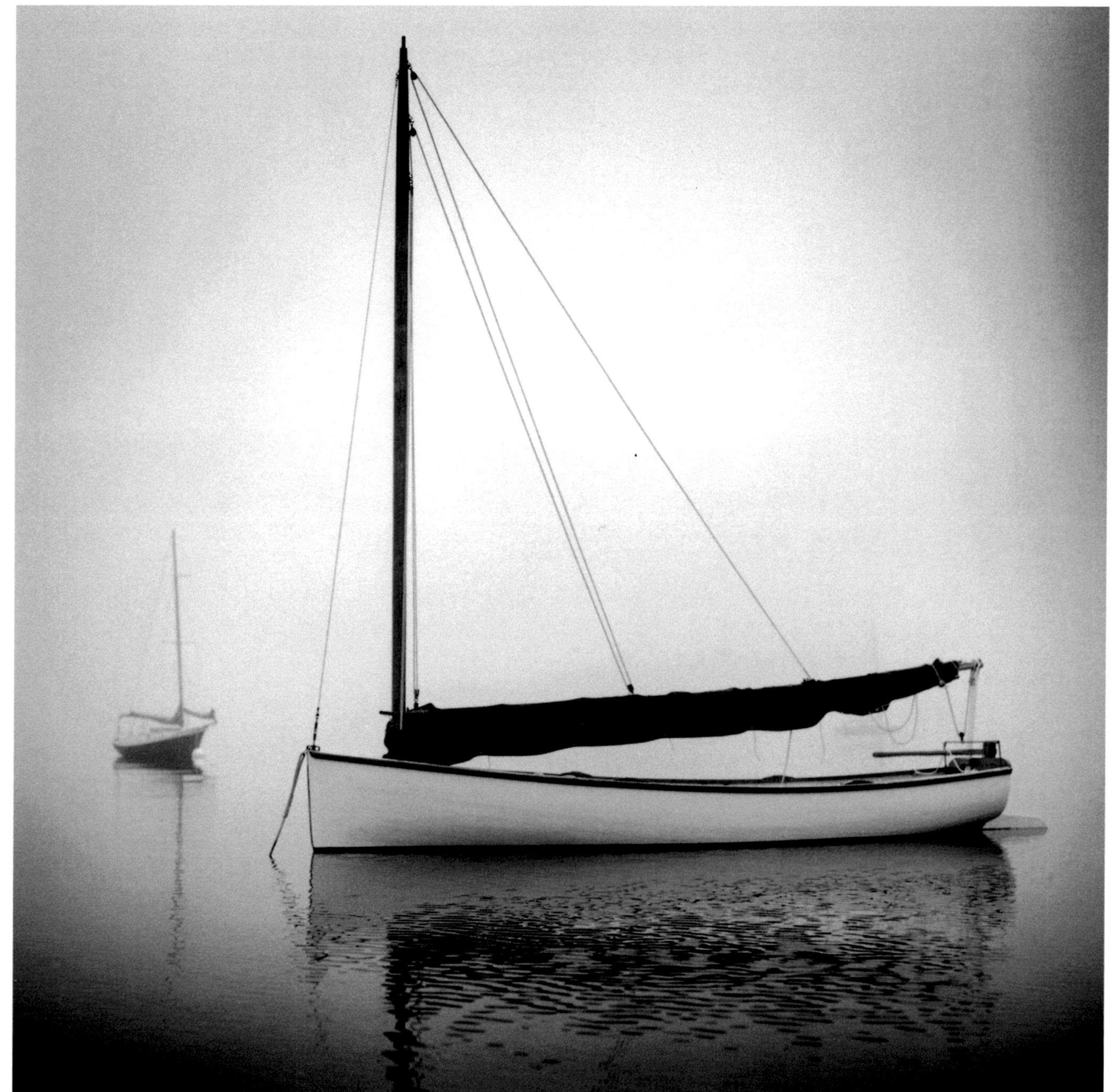

Muriel, 2002

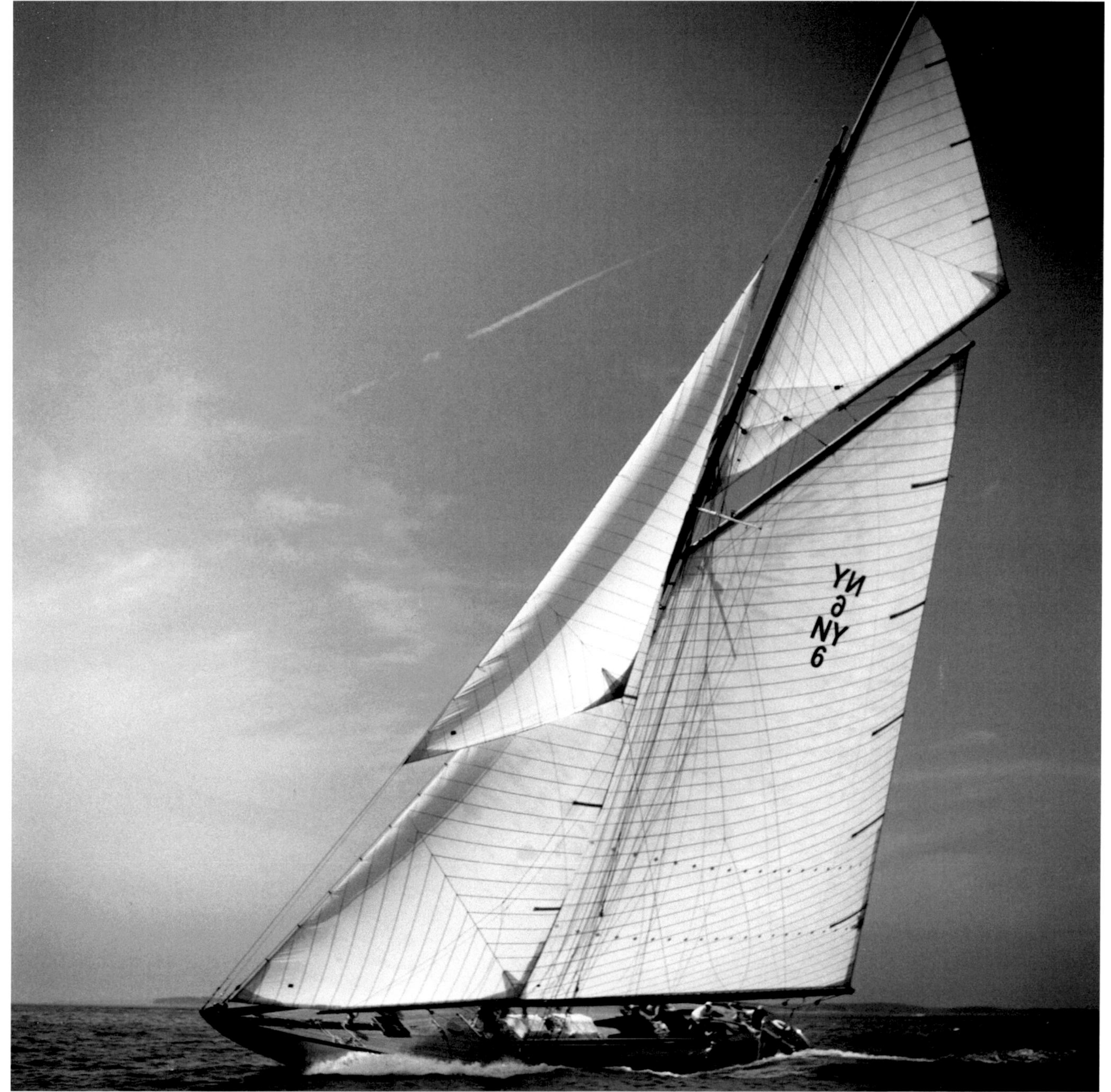

Spartan, 2011

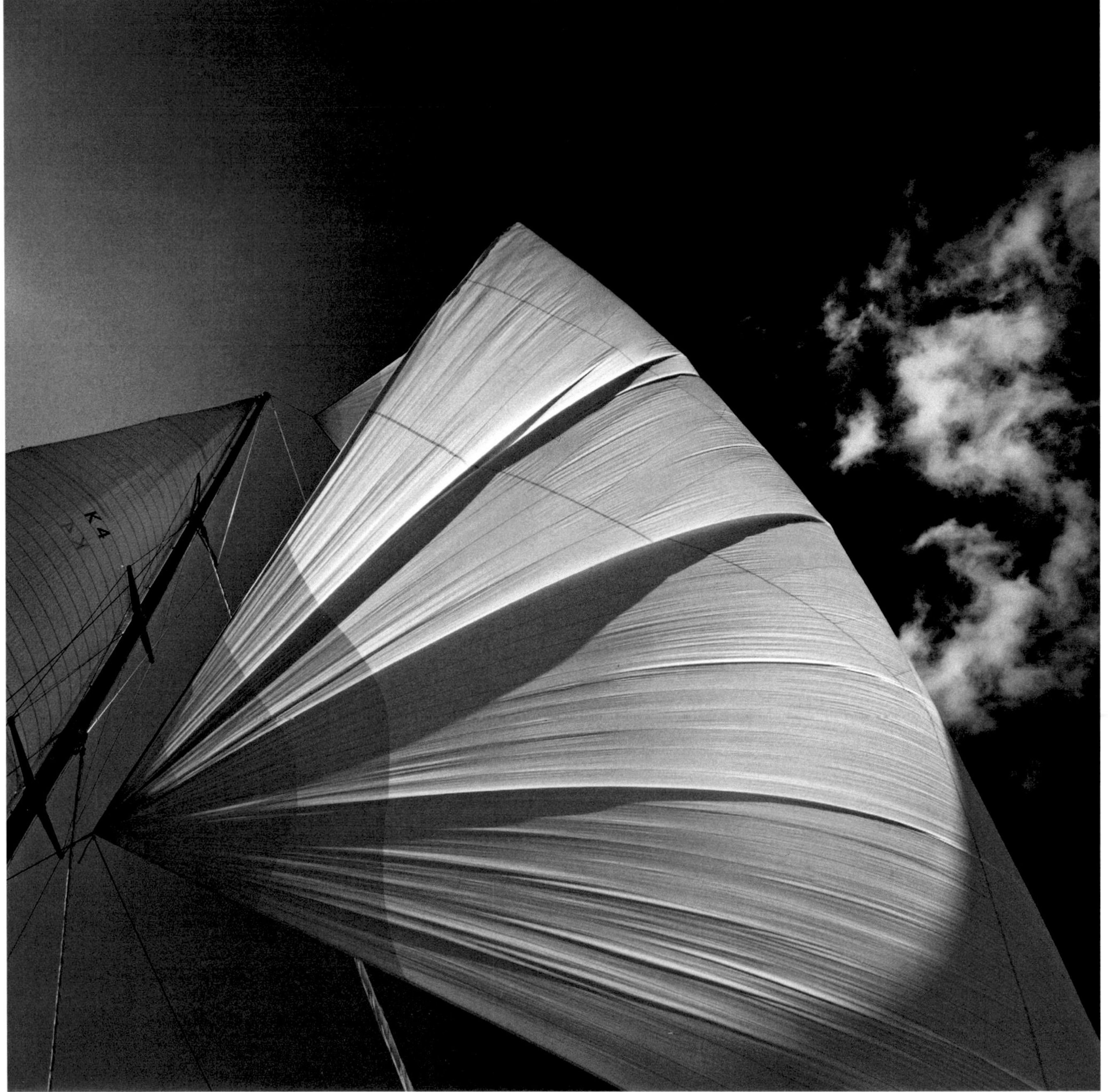

Cambria, 2001

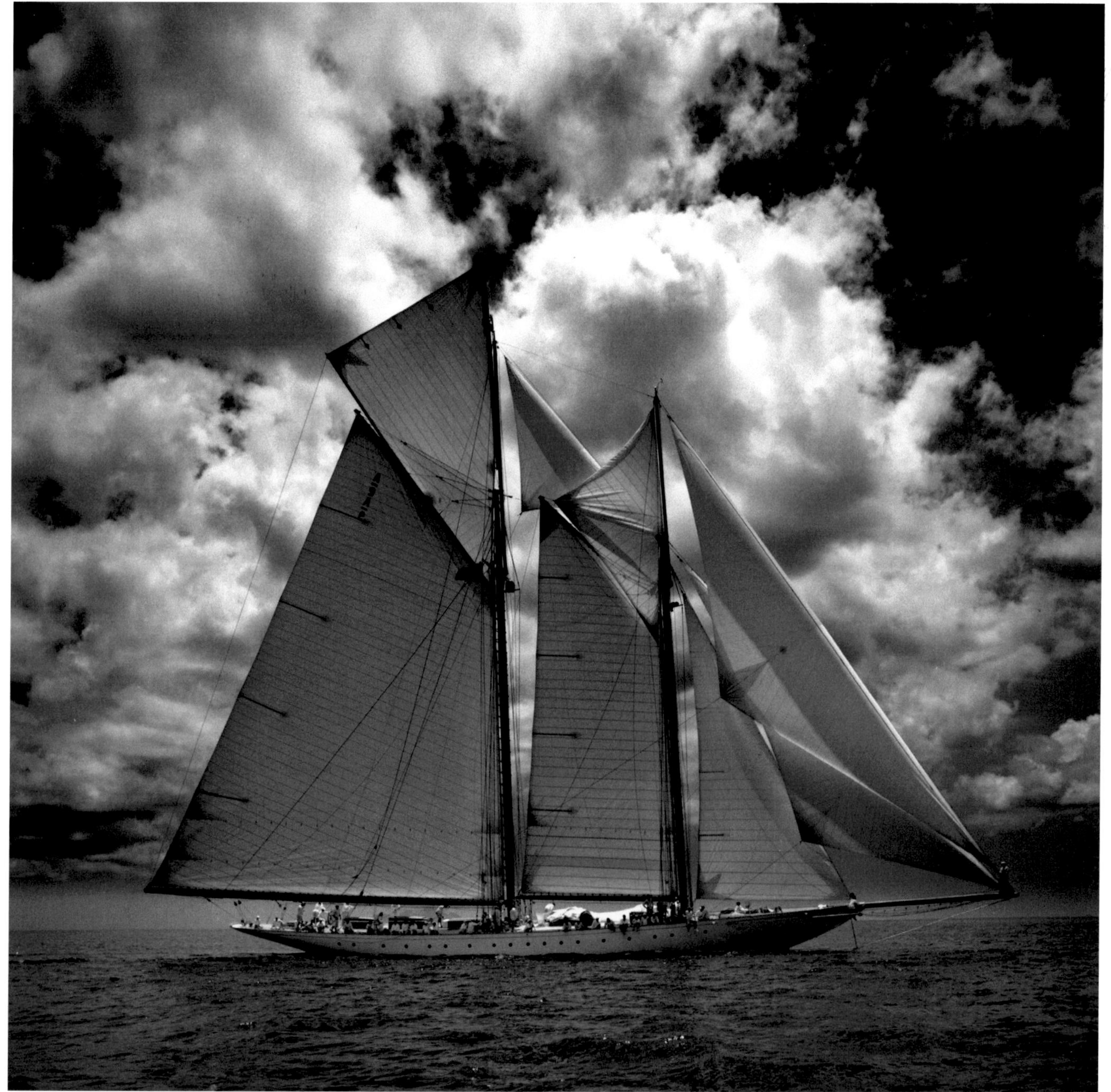

Elena, 2011

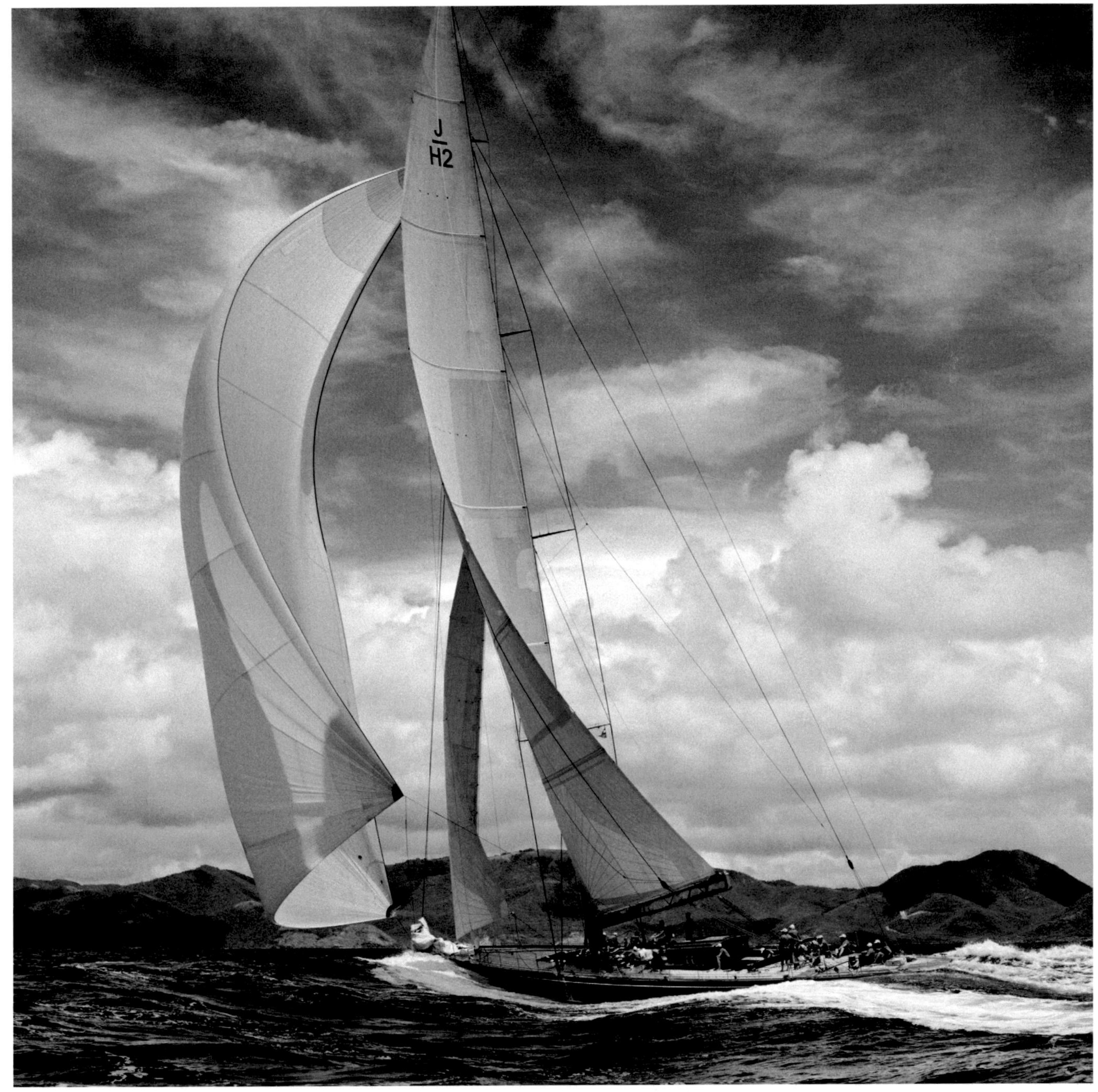

Rainbow, 2015

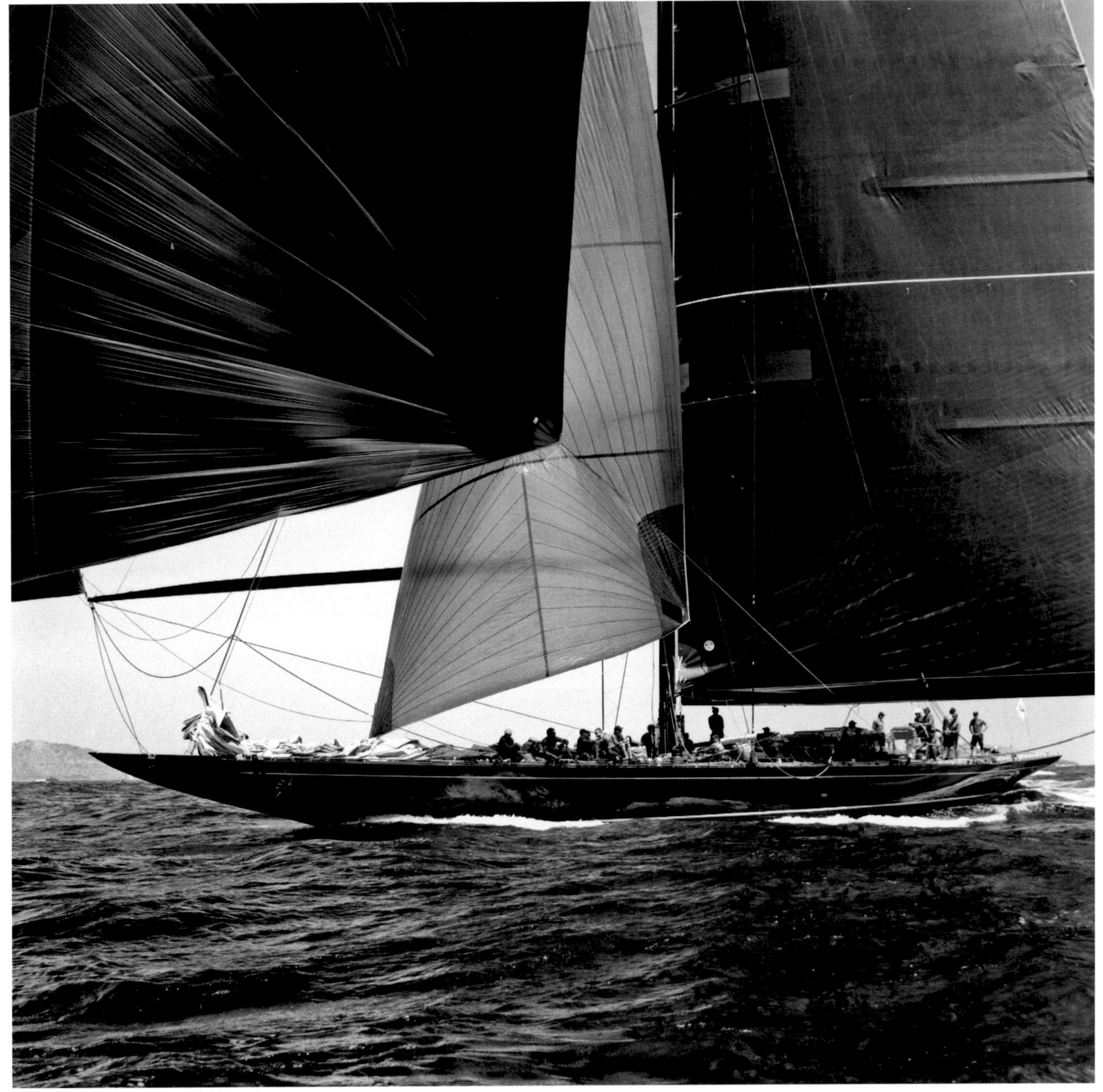

Hanuman, 2017

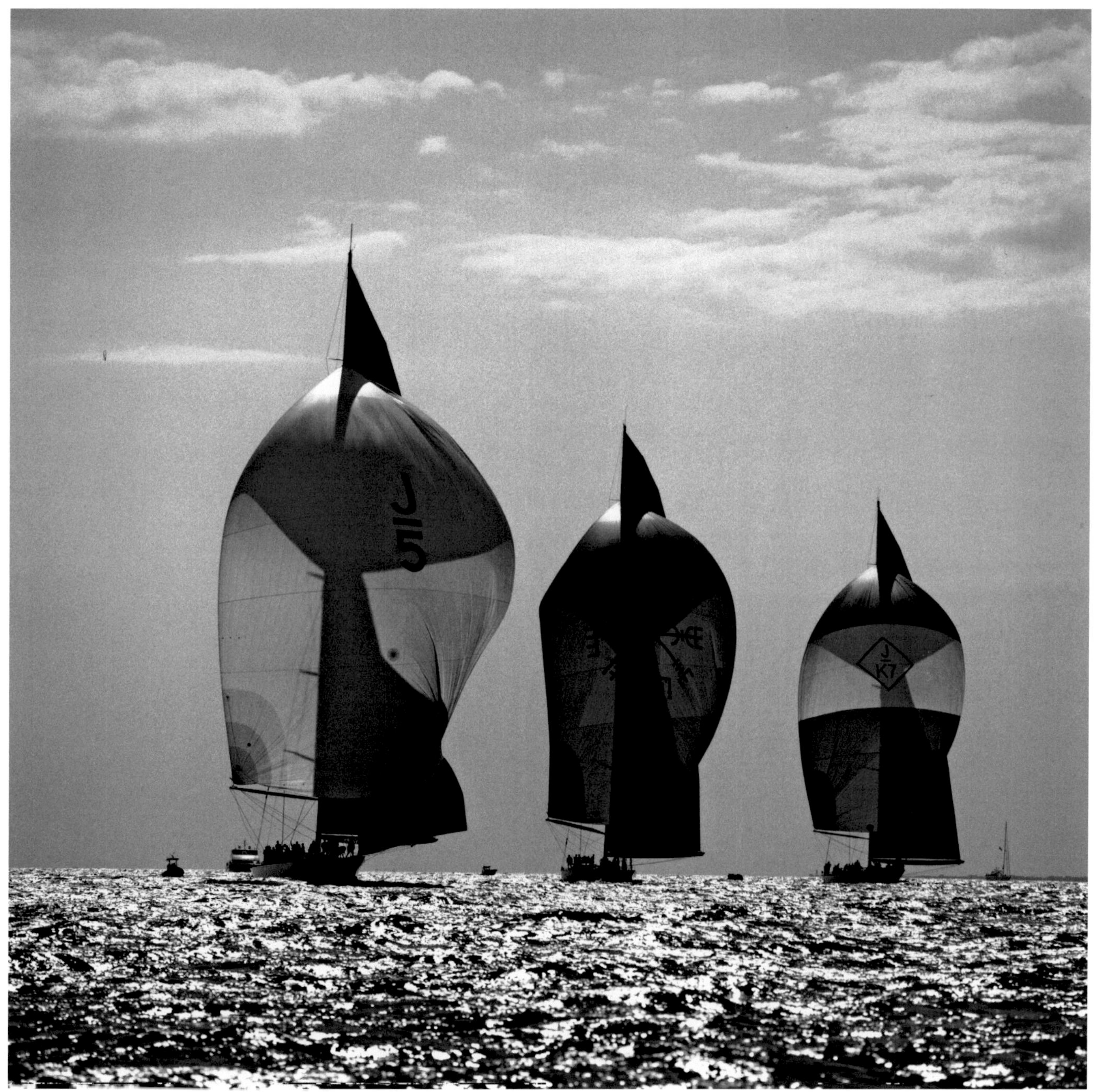

Ranger, Svea, and Velsheda, 2017

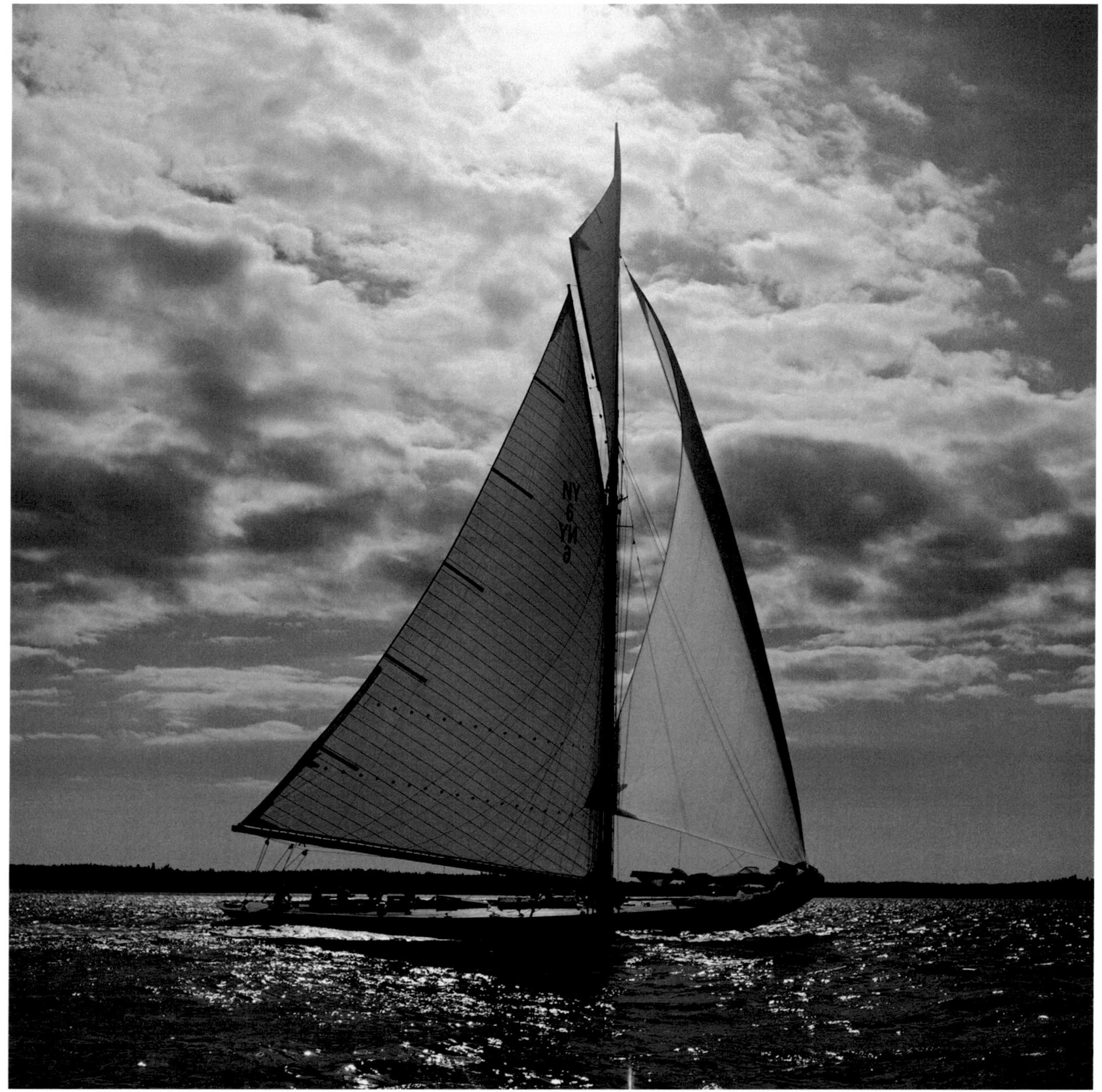

Spartan, 2011

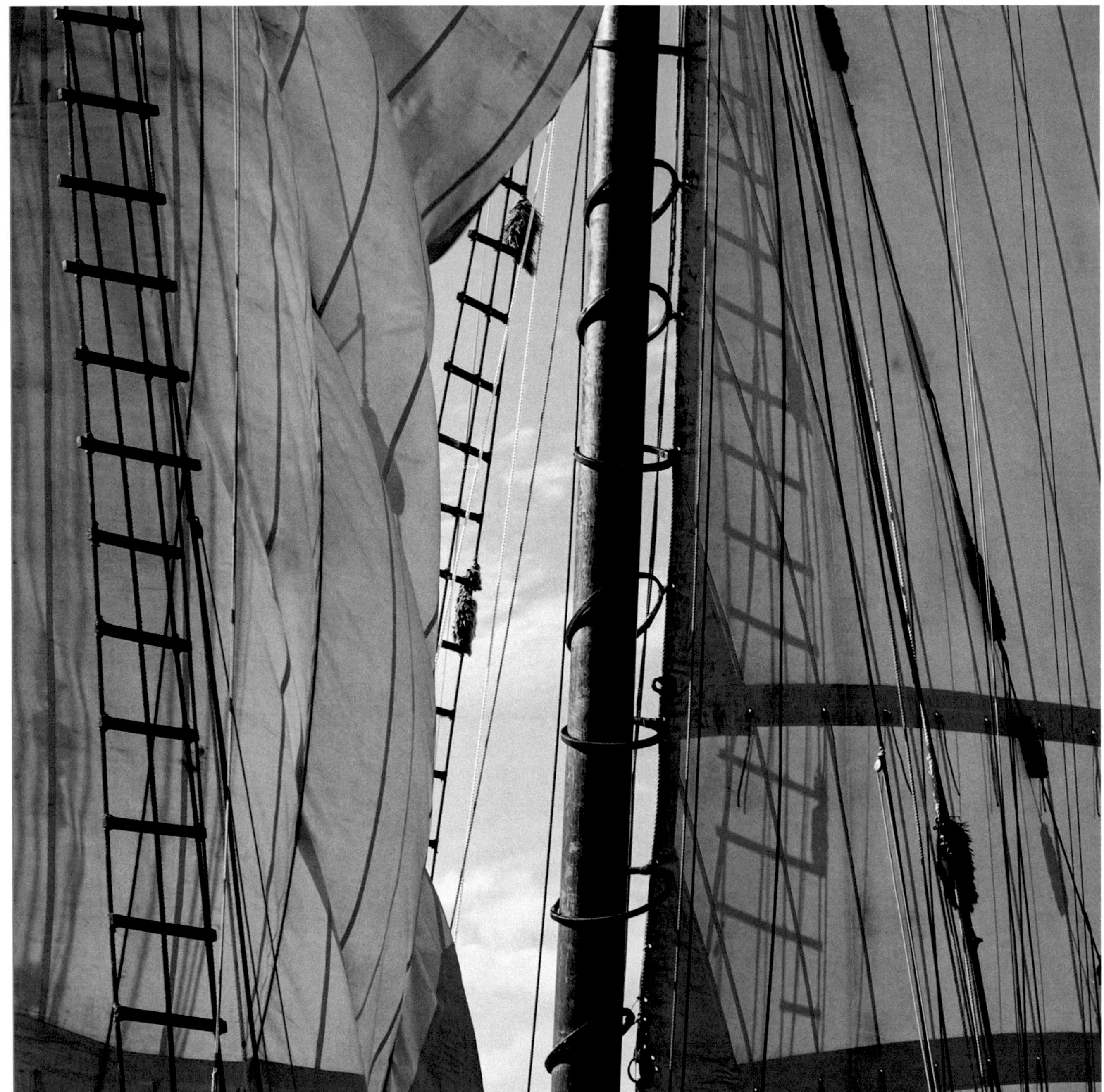

Victory Chimes, 1999

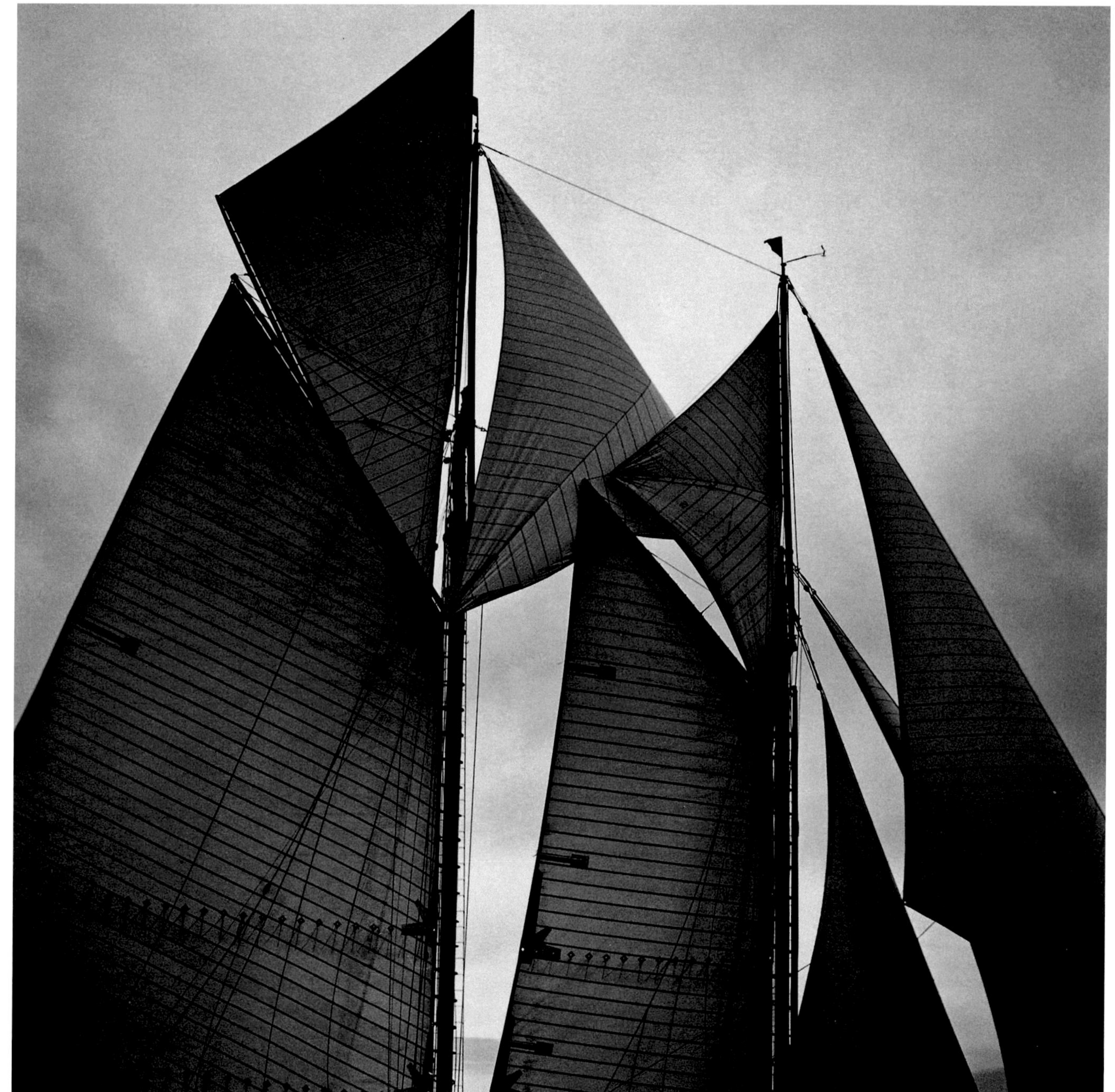

Mariette, 1998

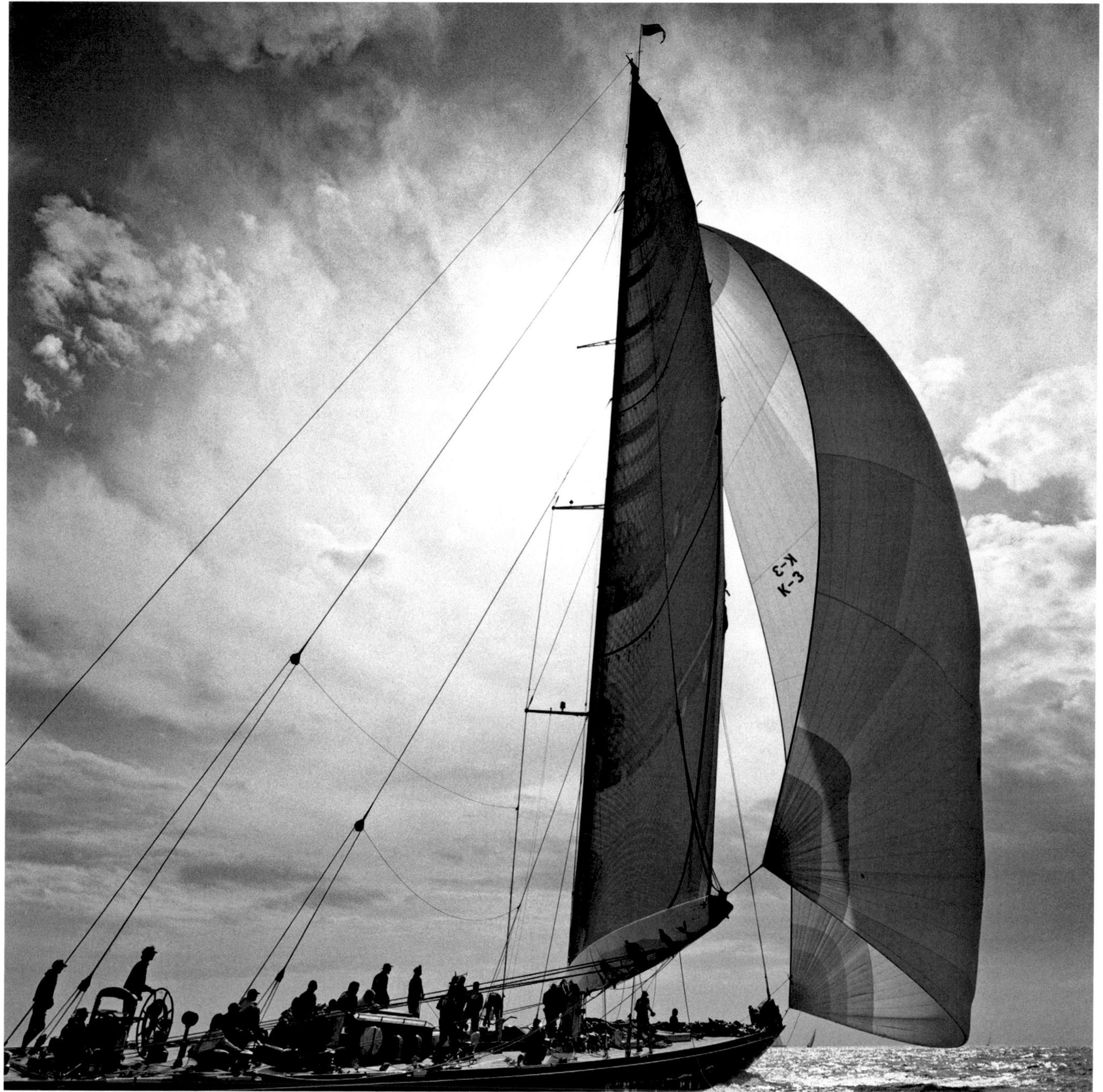

Shamrock V, 2007

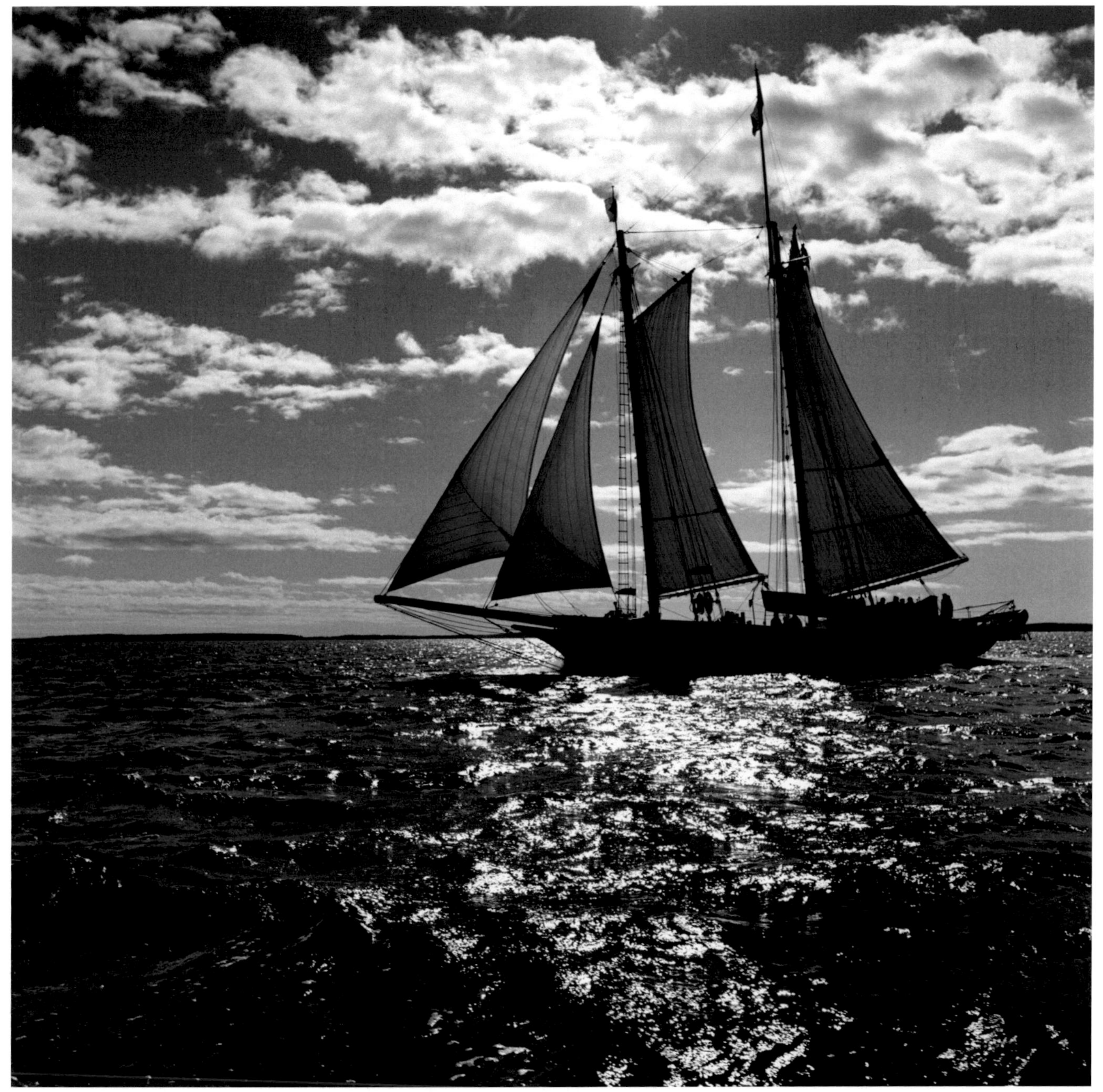

Maine Schooner, 2010

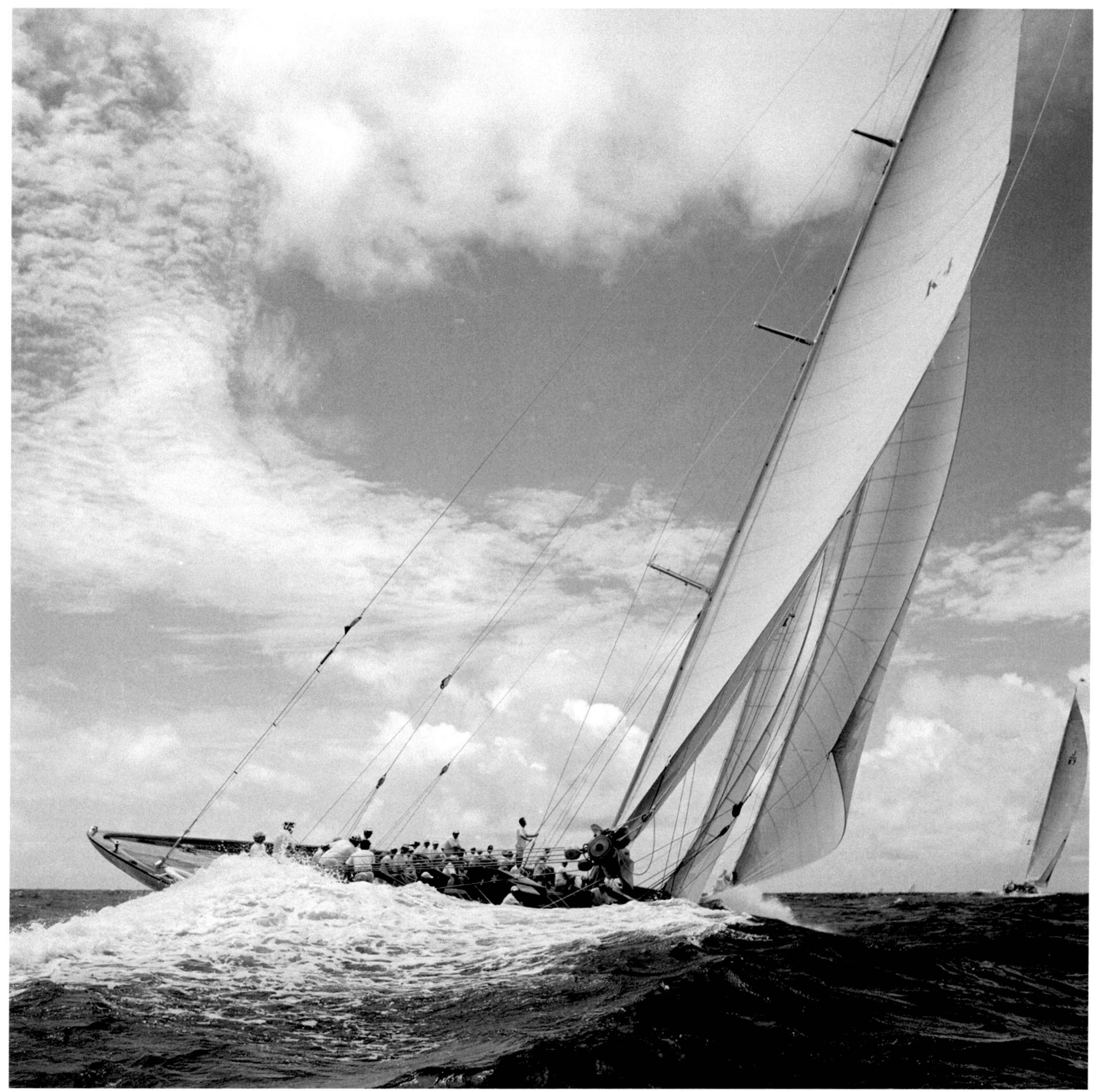

Cambria vs. Endeavour, 2004

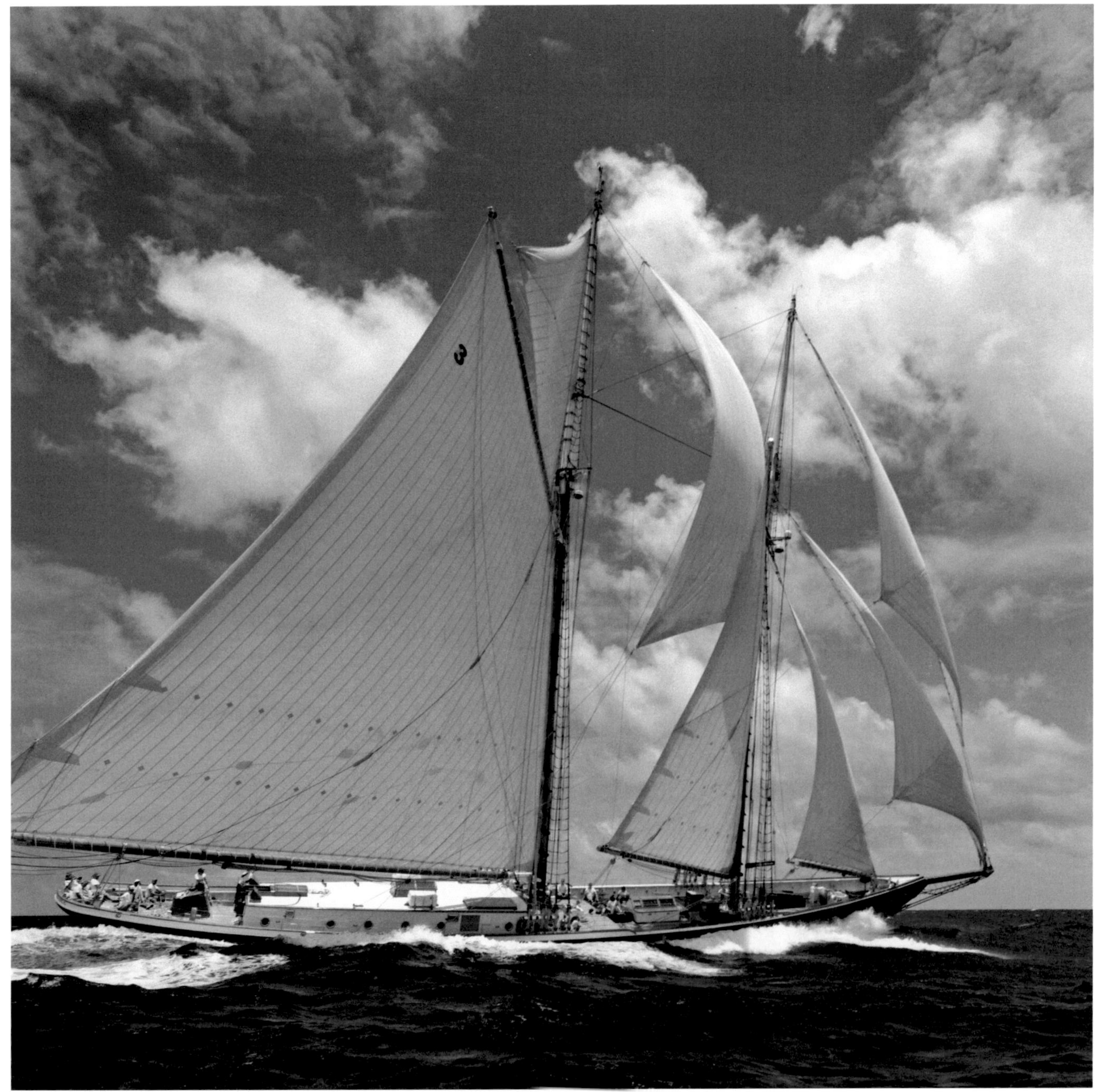

Columbia, 2017

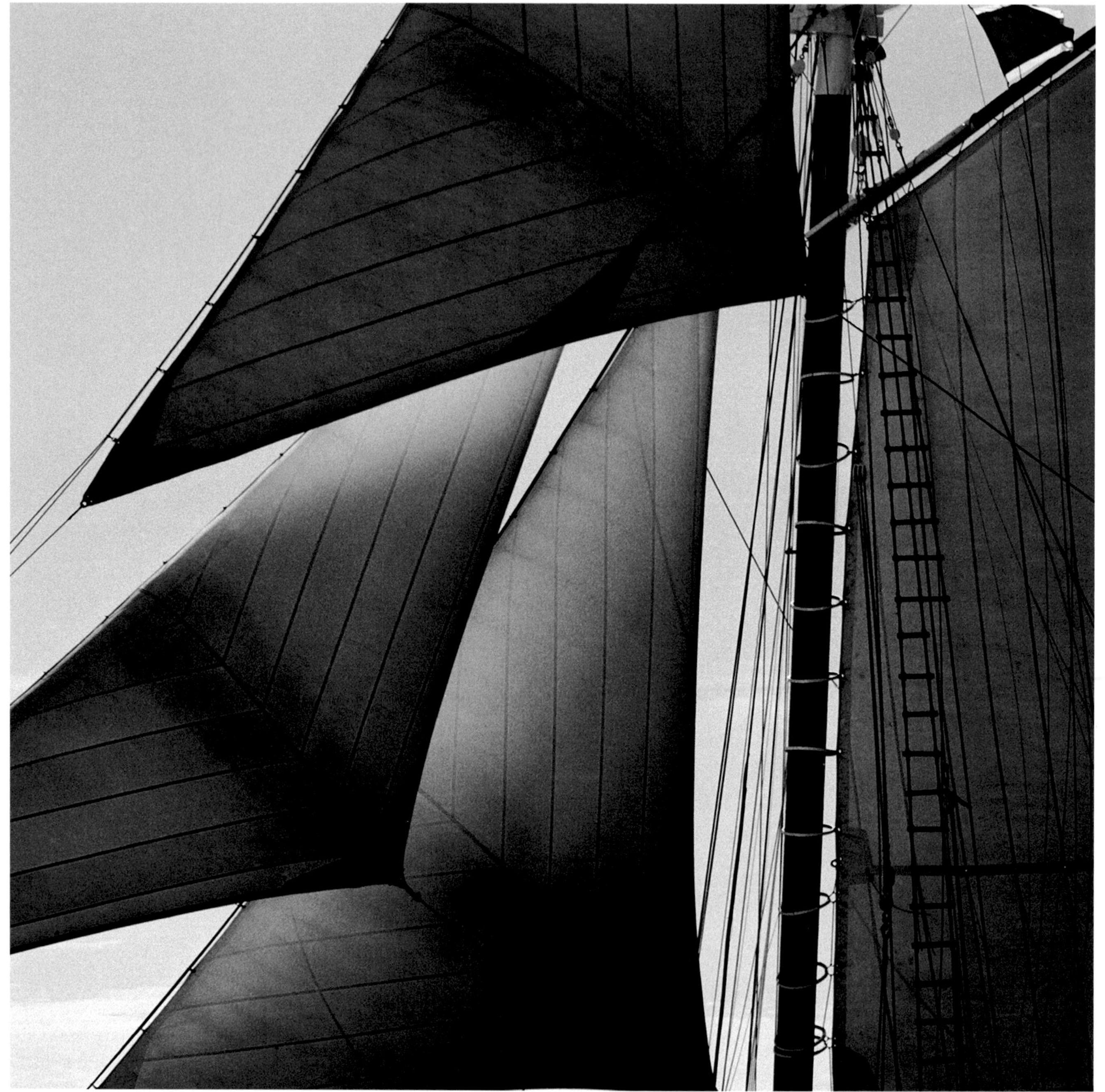

Lewis R. French, 1999

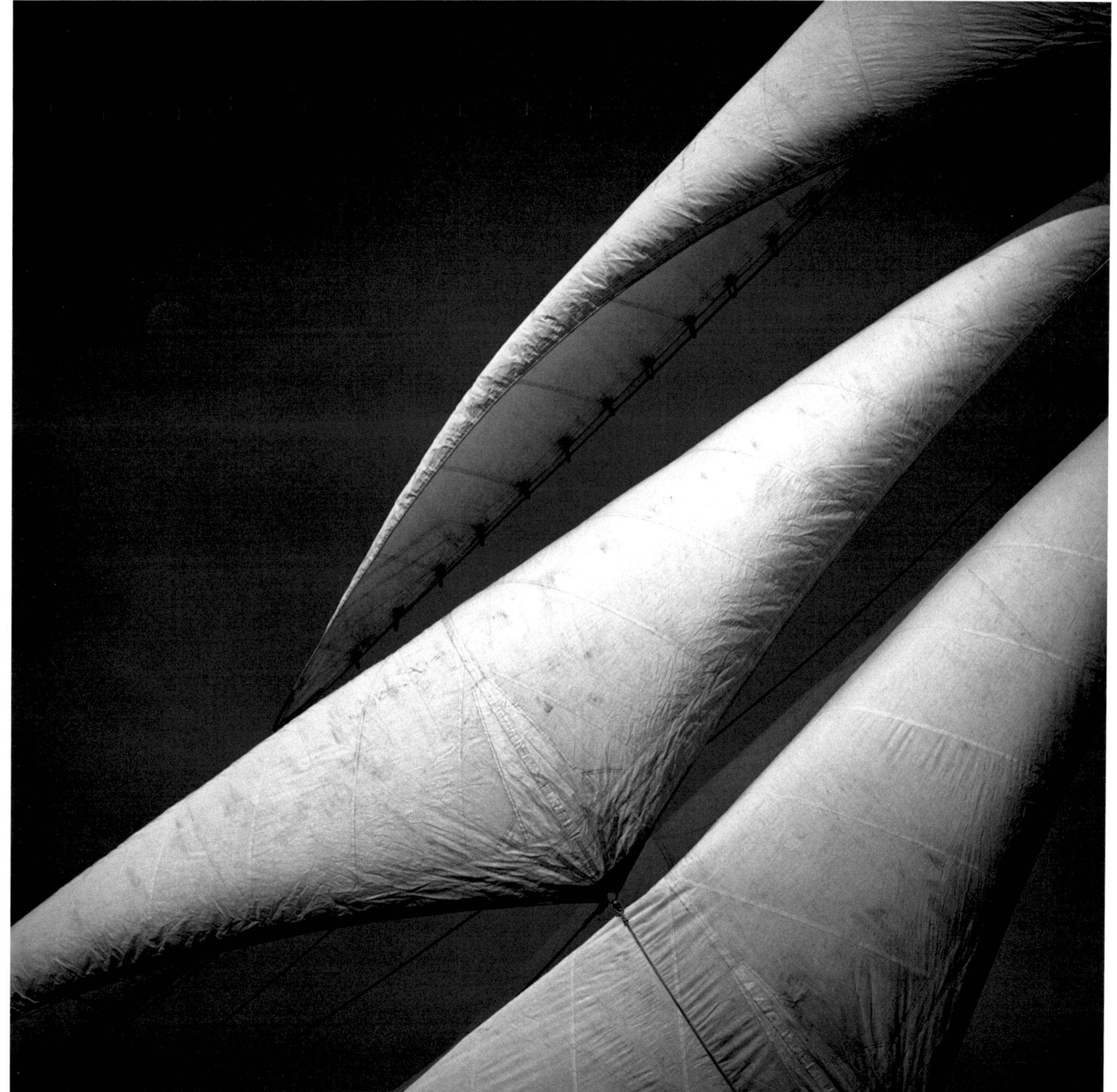

Gloria, 2000

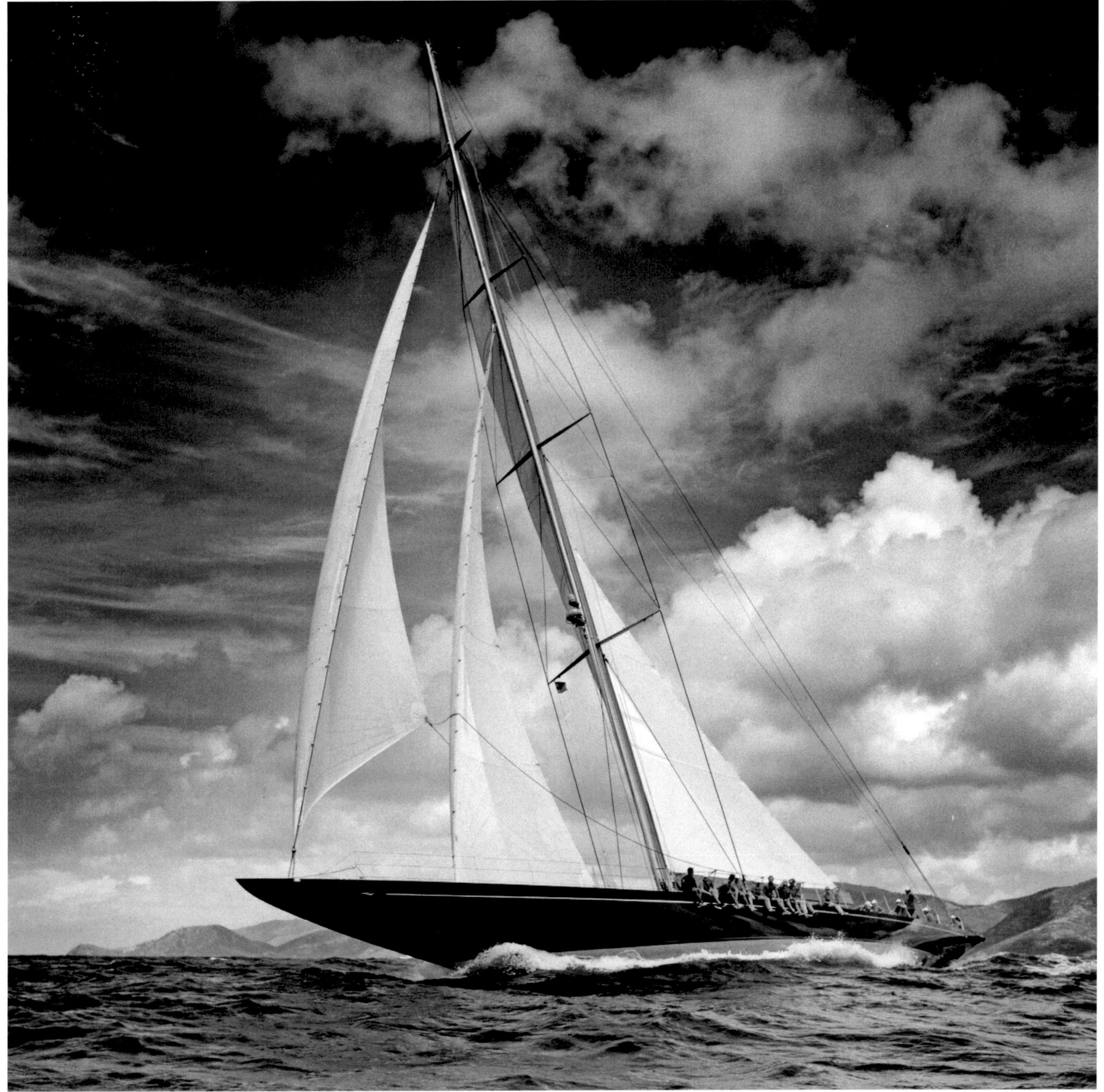

Rainbow, 2015

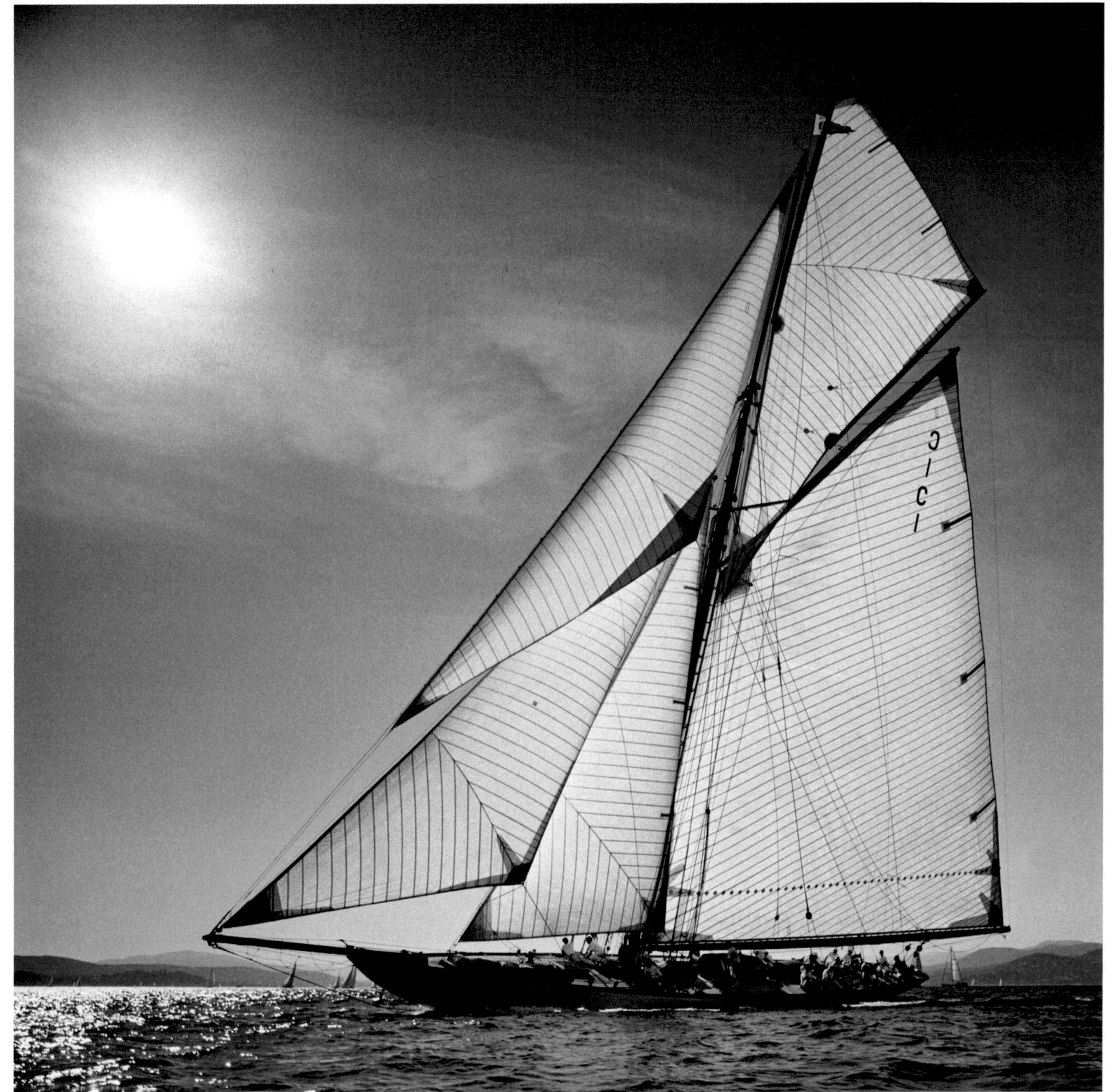

Mariquita, 2007

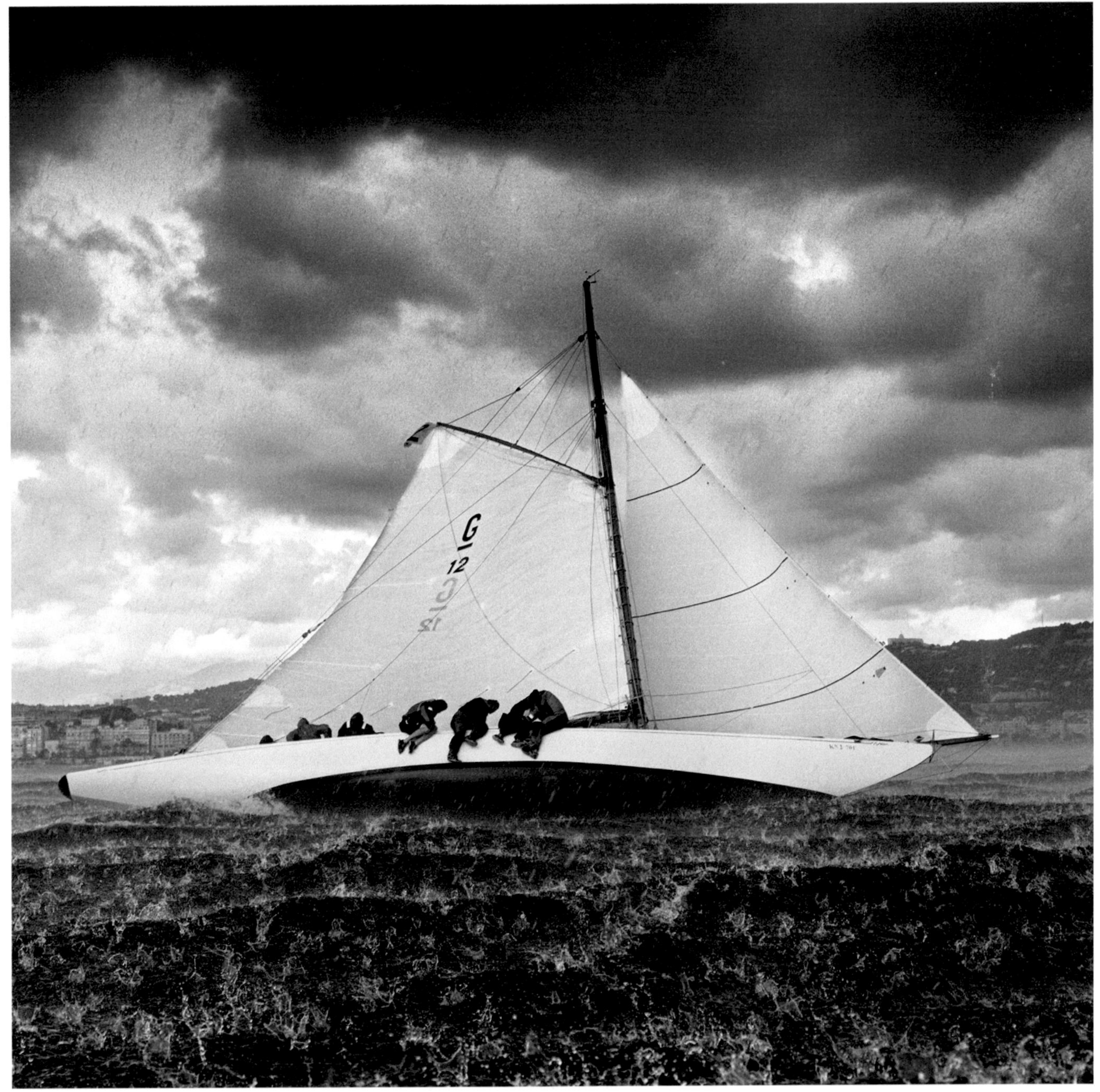

Hailstorm, Cannes, 2007

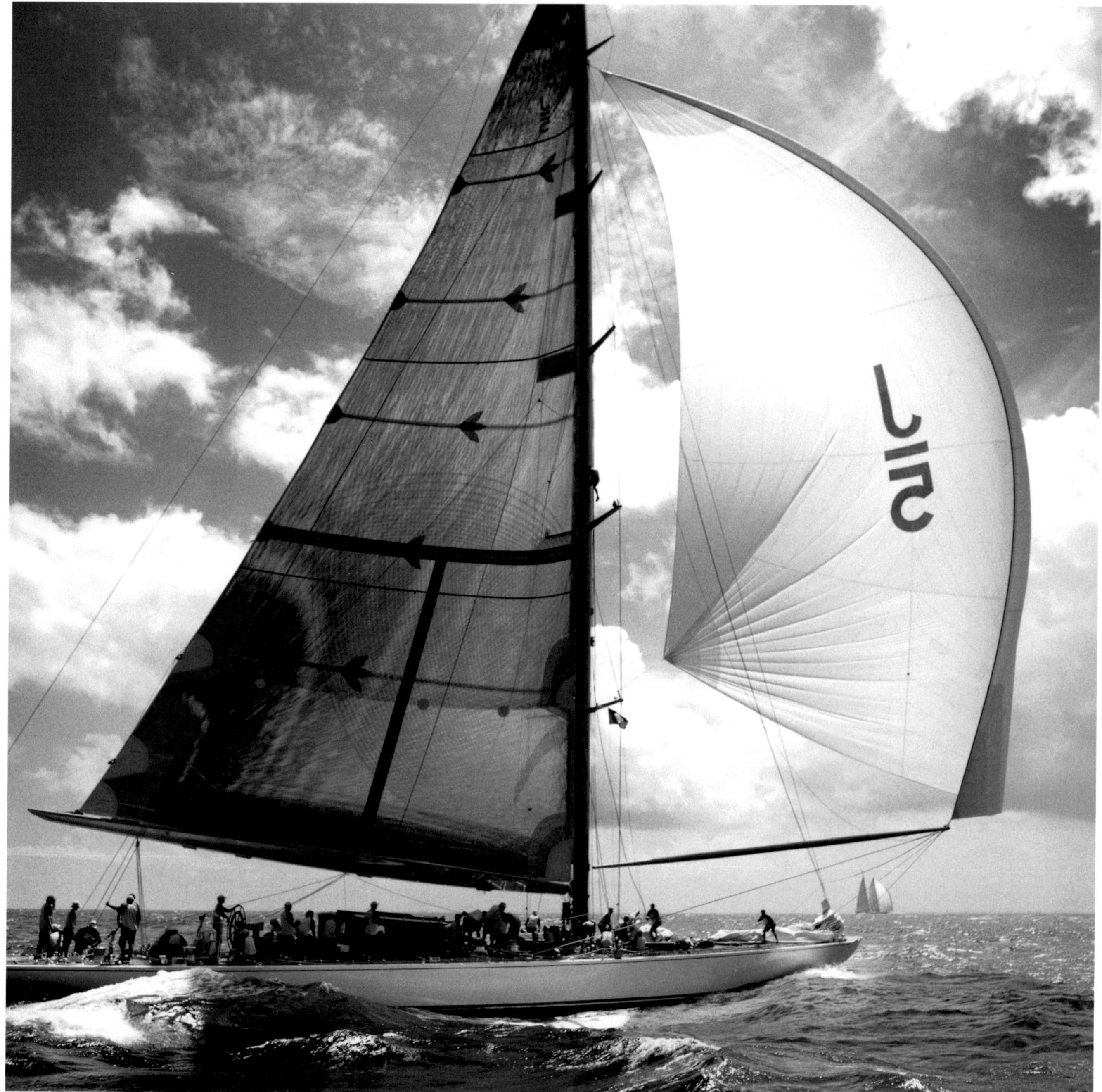

Ranger, 2004

A ship in harbor is safe—
but that is not what ships are built for.

—JOHN A. SHEDD

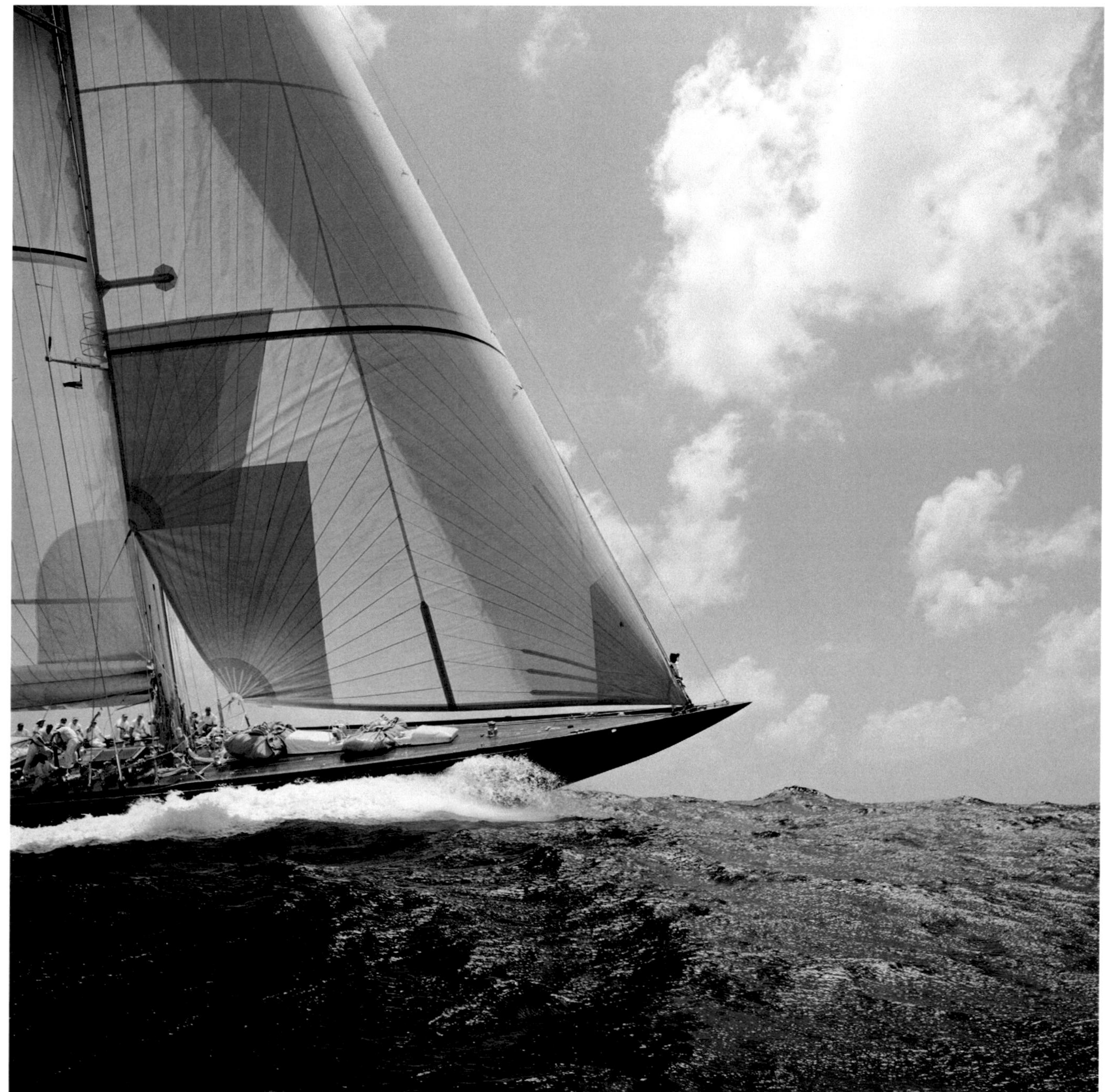

Velsheda, 2001

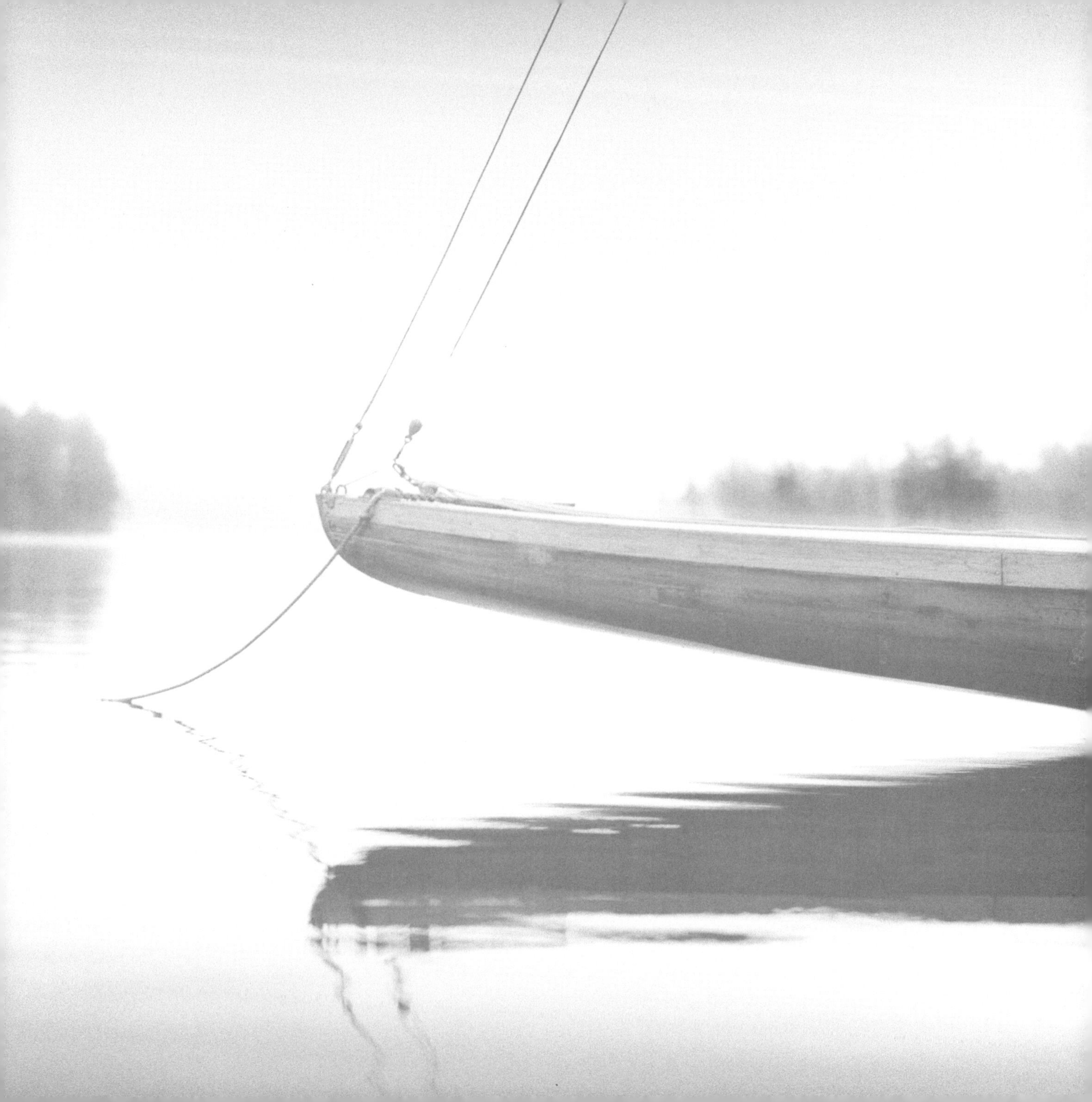

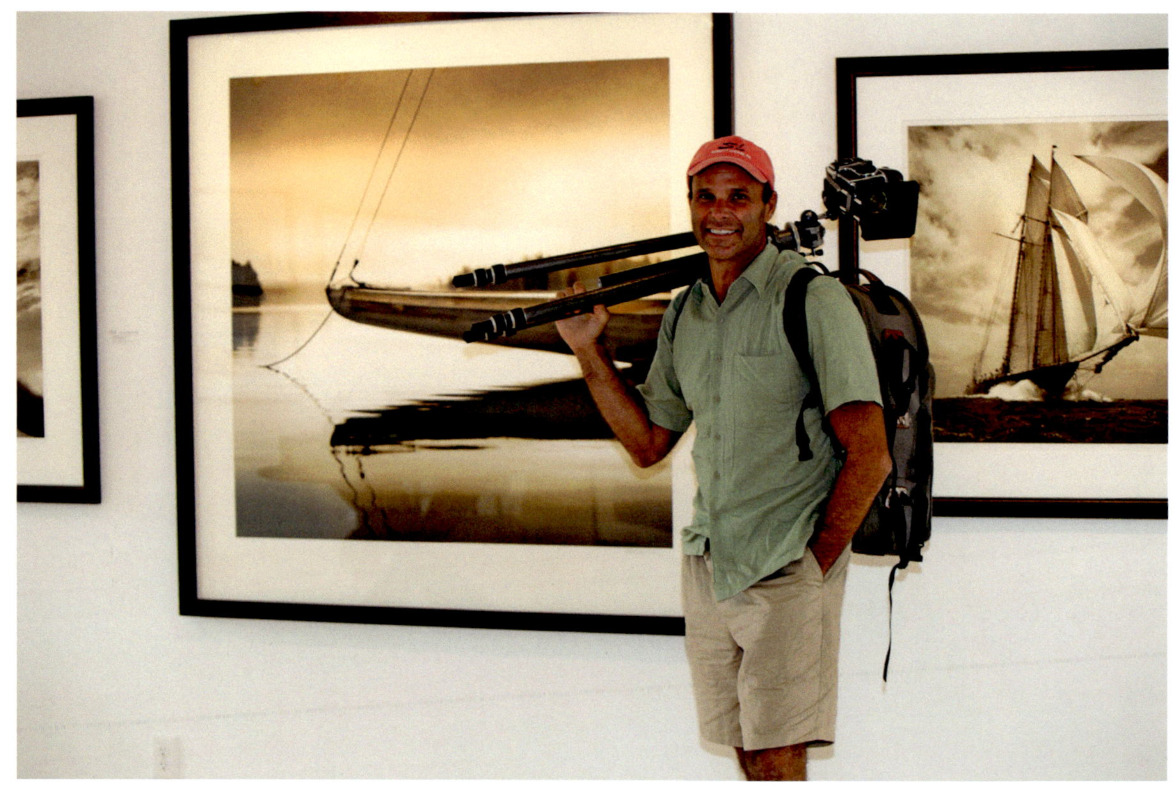

Photo Courtesy of Cindy Vallino, Focus Gallery, Chatham, MA

FOR MORE INFORMATION, PLEASE VISIT

WWW.MICHAELKAHN.COM

MICHAEL KAHN

Michael Kahn learned traditional photography in a portrait studio where they used Hasselblad cameras with a square 6x6 cm film format. Here, Michael received hands-on training in film handling and black-and-white printmaking. Michael continued on in advertising, product, and editorial photography.

In the mid-1990s, Michael took his first sailing photograph of a small boat in the fog on a lake in the Adirondacks, thus beginning his nautical photography career. Making the decision to stay with his film cameras instead of going with the new trends in digital equipment, he makes handmade photographs in his darkroom. Michael continues to travel the world, and his work is widely featured in magazines, museums, corporate and private collections, and fine-art galleries. Michael loves everything about nature and is interested in preservation. His other books are *Brandywine, The Spirit of Sailing,* and *Over the Dunes.*

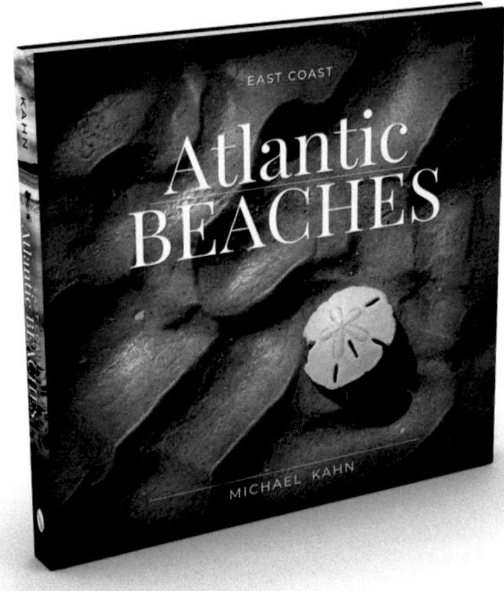

Other Schiffer Books by the Author:

East Coast Atlantic Beaches
ISBN 978-0-7643-5931-6

Other Schiffer Books on Related Subjects:

Archipelago New York, Thomas Halaczinsky
ISBN 978-0-7643-5507-3

Sailing Fascination, Heinrich Hecht
ISBN 978-0-7643-4268-4

Library of Congress Control Number: 2019947431

Designed by Danielle D. Farmer
Cover design by Danielle D. Farmer
Text by Michael Kahn and Christine Yurick
Creative design and input by Christine Yurick
Type set in Playfair Display/Montserratte

ISBN: 978-0-7643-5930-9
Printed in China

Published by Schiffer Publishing, Ltd.
4880 Lower Valley Road
Atglen, PA 19310
Phone: (610) 593-1777; Fax: (610) 593-2002
E-mail: Info@schifferbooks.com
Web: www.schifferbooks.com